CFP® Certification Exam
PRACTICE QUESTION
WORKBOOK

Matthew Brandeburg, CFP®

1,000 Comprehensive
Practice Questions

CONTENTS

GENERAL PRINCIPLES

QUESTIONS

1. Place the following steps of the financial planning process in the correct order:

   (1) Implement the financial plan.
   (2) Establish the client-planner relationship.
   (3) Analyze and evaluate the client's financial status.
   (4) Monitor the financial plan.
   (5) Gather data and determine goals and expectations.
   (6) Develop and present the financial plan.

   A. 2, 3, 5, 6, 1, 4
   B. 2, 5, 3, 6, 1, 4
   C. 2, 5, 3, 1, 6, 4
   D. 5, 2, 3, 6, 1, 4

2. According to the Principle of _____, a **CFP®** Board designee shall not solicit clients through false or misleading communications or advertisements.

   A. Fairness
   B. Professionalism
   C. Integrity
   D. Objectivity

3. Which of the following is not one of the forms of discipline that may be imposed by the **CFP®** Board if grounds for discipline have been established against a **CFP®** Board designee?

   A. Require additional continuing education hours in any subject matter areas separate from, or in addition to, any form of discipline.
   B. Issue a public letter of admonition.
   C. Permanently revoke the right to use the CFP® mark.
   D. All of the above are possible forms of discipline.

4. If an RIA has more than _____ of assets under management, the RIA must register with the SEC.

    A. $20 million
    B. $25 million
    C. $30 million
    D. $35 million

5. Renee wants to deposit an amount today that will last for 6 years. She needs to withdraw $1,400 at the beginning of each 6-month period and expects to earn 12% compounded semiannually on her investments. How much does Renee need to deposit today to achieve her goal?

    A. $10,673.59
    B. $11,737.38
    C. $12,441.62
    D. $13,889.23

6. According to the Principle of Confidentiality, a CFP® Board designee shall treat client information as confidential, except:

(1) as required in response to proper legal process.
(2) as needed to establish an advisory or brokerage account.
(3) to defend against charges of wrongdoing.
(4) in connection with a civil dispute between the CFP® Board designee and the client.

    A. (1) and (2) only
    B. (3) and (4) only
    C. (1), (3), and (4) only
    D. All of the above

7.Which of the following are included as part of the financial planning step "Establish the client-planner relationship"?

(1) Identify the services to be provided.
(2) Identify activities necessary for implementation.
(3) Coordinate the financial plan with other professionals.
(4) Determine the roles and responsibilities of the client and financial planner.

A. (2) and (3) only
B. (1) and (4) only
C. (1), (3), and (4) only
D. All of the above

8. Jenny has been investing $2,000 at the end of each year for the past 11 years. How much has she accumulated, assuming she has earned 8% compounded annually on her investments?

A. $31,228.90
B. $33,290.97
C. $35,954.25
D. $37,840.32

9. David had five credit cards in his wallet when it was stolen on the subway. The credit cards were fraudulently used before he could report them missing. He provides you with the following amounts that were charged against each card and asks you to determine his liability. What is David's total liability for these transactions?

Card 1: $50
Card 2: $800
Card 3: $475
Card 4: $30
Card 5: $450

A. $0
B. $50
C. $230
D. $1,805

10. According to the Principle of _____ , a CFP® Board designee shall not commingle client funds or other property with a CFP® Board designee's personal funds and/or other property of a CFP® Board designee's firm.

   A. Integrity
   B. Objectivity
   C. Confidentiality
   D. Diligence

11. Tracy's bond has a market price of $910. The bond pays an 11% coupon and will mature in 6 years. What is the bond's yield to maturity?

   A. 13.22%
   B. 14.59%
   C. 15.27%
   D. 16.12%

12. Consumer debt payments, such as credit cards and vehicle loans, should not exceed _____ of _____ income.

   A. 20%, gross
   B. 20%, net
   C. 28%, gross
   D. 28%, net

13. Housing debt costs, including principal, interest, taxes, and insurance, should not exceed _____ of _____ income.

   A. 20%, gross
   B. 20%, net
   C. 28%, gross
   D. 28%, net

14. Total debt payment should not exceed _____ of _____ income.

   A. 28%, gross
   B. 28%, net
   C. 36%, gross
   D. 36%, net

15. Which of the following are qualified expenses to be paid from a 529 plan?

   (1) Books
   (2) Tuition
   (3) Supplies
   (4) Room and board

   A. (1) and (3) only
   B. (1), (2), and (3) only
   C. (2), (3), and (4) only
   D. All of the above

16. **Jim, John, and Jerry would each like to contribute money to their nephew's Coverdell Education Savings Account (ESA). Which of the following is correct regarding the maximum contribution that can be made on behalf of the nephew?**

   A. Jim, John, and Jerry are permitted to contribute a combined amount not to exceed $2,000 into their nephew's ESA in the current year.
   B. Jim, John, and Jerry are permitted to each contribute $2,000 into their nephew's ESA in the current year, for a total annual contribution of $6,000.
   C. Jim, John, and Jerry may each contribute up to the annual gift tax exclusion amount into their nephew's ESA in the current year.
   D. Jim, John, and Jerry may "front-load" contributions into their nephew's ESA, so each may contribute up to five times the annual gift tax exclusion amount in the current year.

For questions 17-19, match the economic policy with the description that follows. Use only one answer per blank. Answers may be used more than once or not at all.

    A. Expansionary policy
    B. Contractionary policy

17. _____ **Taxes increase**

18. _____ **Public spending increases**

19. _____ **Government borrowing decreases**

20. **Which of the following are characteristics of Pell Grants?**

    (1) Only full-time students are eligible
    (2) Distributed on the basis of financial need and availability of federal funds
    (3) Receipt of other grants and loans is contingent upon applying for or receiving Pell funds
    (4) Available to undergraduate and graduate students

    A. (1) and (4) only
    B. (2) and (3) only
    C. (1), (2), and (3) only
    D. All of the above

21. **Charlie purchased a rare baseball card for $600. He kept the baseball card for 5 years before selling it. If the internal rate of return for the 5-year period was 9%, what was the final selling price?**

    A. $923.17
    B. $926.39
    C. $930.28
    D. $933.40

22. **All but which of the following are correct regarding Federal Supplemental Educational Opportunity Grants (SEOGs)?**

    A. Funded by the federal government, but administered by individual schools
    B. Available to undergraduate students only
    C. Available to full-time students only
    D. Distributed on the basis of financial need

23. **Stafford Loans are administered by the:**

    A. Private Loan Administration (PLA).
    B. Federal Family Education Loan Program (FFELP).
    C. Parent Loans to Undergraduate Students (PLUS).
    D. Federal Assistance Loan Program (FALP).

24. **Which of the following are characteristics of Perkins loans?**

    (1) Repayment may be extended to 10 years
    (2) Available to undergraduate students only
    (3) Both full-time and part-time students are eligible
    (4) Distributed on the basis of financial need

    A. (1), (2), and (4) only
    B. (1), (3), and (4) only
    C. (2), (3), and (4) only
    D. All of the above

25. **All but which of the following are correct regarding Parent Loans to Undergraduate Students (PLUS)?**

    A. Both full-time and part-time students are eligible
    B. Loans are not based on financial need
    C. Available to parents of undergraduate students up to the cost of attendance at the institution minus additional financial support
    D. All of the above are correct.

26. Which of the following are correct regarding the laws of supply and demand?

(1) The law of demand demonstrates an inverse relationship between the price consumers are willing to pay for a product and the amount they are willing to purchase.
(2) Consumers are more responsive to price when substitutes are available.
(3) The demand curve slopes down and to the right, indicating that as price decreases, the quantity demanded increases.
(4) The demand curve slopes down and to the left, indicating that as price decreases, the quantity demanded decreases.

A. (1) and (2) only
B. (1), (2), and (3) only
C. (2), (3), and (4) only
D. All of the above

27. When a small change in price causes a large change in the quantity purchased, the product is considered to be _____.

A. elastic
B. inelastic
C. durable
D. non-durable

28. What is the current price of a zero-coupon bond with a $1,000 face value, a YTM of 8.46%, and 5 years until maturity?

A. $620.47
B. $640.18
C. $660.80
D. $680.28

29. **All but which of the following are correct regarding price inelasticity?**

    A. Inelastic products have many available substitutes.
    B. It results when a large change in price has only a small impact on the quantity demanded.
    C. An example of an inelastic product is gasoline.
    D. All of the above are correct.

30. **Perfect elasticity results in a _____ demand curve. Perfect inelasticity results in a _____ demand curve.**

    A. vertical, horizontal
    B. horizontal, vertical
    C. diagonal, horizontal
    D. vertical, diagonal

31. **What is the current market price of a bond that pays a 10% coupon and matures in 8 years? Comparable bonds are yielding 12.6%.**

    A. $489.04
    B. $710.18
    C. $871.29
    D. $999.99

32. **Money in a Coverdell Education Savings Account (ESA) must be used by the time the beneficiary is _____ years of age.**

    A. 18
    B. 21
    C. 24
    D. 30

33. According to the Second Law of Demand, when the price of a product increases, consumers will reduce their consumption more in the _____ than in the _____. Thus, the demand for products is more _____ in the long run than in the short run.

    A. short run, long run, elastic
    B. short run, long run, inelastic
    C. long run, short run, elastic
    D. long run, short run, inelastic

34. Jane purchased a rare stamp collection for $30,000. She expects it will increase in value at a rate of 12% compounded annually for the next 4 years. How much will her stamp collection be worth at the end of the fourth year if her expectations are correct?

    A. $37,212.44
    B. $41,310.98
    C. $47,205.58
    D. $55,210.12

35. Which of the following will cause a shift in the demand curve?

    (1) Change in consumer income
    (2) Change in the price of complement and substitute goods
    (3) Change in consumer expectations
    (4) Change in consumer tastes and preferences

    A. (1) only
    B. (2) and (4) only
    C. (2), (3), and (4) only
    D. All of the above

36. A change in quantity supplied is identified by which of the following?

A. Shifting the demand curve
B. Shifting the supply curve
C. Movement along the supply curve
D. Movement along the demand curve

For questions 37-43, match the economic indicator with the description that follows. Use only one answer per blank. Answers may be used more than once or not at all.

A. Leading economic indicator
B. Lagging economic indicator

37. ____ Change in consumer sentiment

38. ____ Average prime rate charged by banks

39. ____ Change in the Consumer Price Index (CPI)

40. ____ Orders for durable goods

41. ____ Average duration of unemployment

42. ____ Change in money supply

43. ____ Housing starts

44. According to the Principle of _____, a CFP® Board designee shall disclose conflicts of interest and sources of compensation.

A. Fairness
B. Objectivity
C. Confidentiality
D. Professionalism

45. What is the maximum contribution a donor can make in a single year to a 529 plan if the gift tax annual exclusion is $13,000? Assume the donor has not made previous contributions to a 529 plan.

A. $13,000
B. $26,000
C. $65,000
D. $100,000

46. Carrie wants to accumulate $95,000 in 7.5 years to purchase a rental property. She expects to earn an annual rate of 9.5% compounded quarterly. How much does Carrie need to invest today to achieve her goal?

A. $46,979.26
B. $48,292.38
C. $49,840.25
D. $50,283.49

47. Which of the following may cause a shift in the supply curve?

(1) Change in resource prices
(2) Change in technology
(3) Natural disaster
(4) Political disruption

A. (1) and (2) only
B. (2) and (3) only
C. (2), (3), and (4) only
D. All of the above

48. Devin sued his former employer and won a judgment that provides him $2,000 at the end of each 6-month period for the next 5 years. If the account that hold's Devin's settlement earns an average annual rate of 7% compounded semiannually, how much was the employer initially required to pay Devin?

A. $15,328.29
B. $16,633.21
C. $17,215.37
D. $18,108.38

49. Place the Principles of the Code of Ethics in the correct order:

(1) The Principle of Fairness
(2) The Principle of Competence
(3) The Principle of Integrity
(4) The Principle of Professionalism
(5) The Principle of Objectivity
(6) The Principle of Diligence
(7) The Principle of Confidentiality

A. 3, 2, 5, 4, 7, 6, 1
B. 2, 5, 7, 4, 1, 3, 6
C. 3, 5, 2, 1, 7, 4, 6
D. 5, 2, 4, 7, 6, 3, 1

50. Sarah expects to receive $150,000 from an irrevocable trust in 7 years. What is the current value of the trust if it is earning an annual rate of 10% compounded quarterly?

A. $75,131.67
B. $76,274.38
C. $83,485.10
D. $84,273.10

51. To establish a Coverdell Education Savings Account (ESA), the beneficiary must be under age _____ unless the individual is designated as a special needs beneficiary.

    A. 14
    B. 18
    C. 21
    D. 30

52. Michelle has been investing $2,000 at the end of each 6-month period to accumulate funds for her daughter's college tuition. If the funds are earning an annual rate of 6% compounded semiannually, how much will the account be worth when Michelle's daughter begins college in 7 years?

    A. $28,384.06
    B. $29,235.58
    C. $34,172.65
    D. $35,197.83

53. Jacob would like to receive the equivalent of $40,000 in today's dollars at the beginning of each year for the next 8 years. He assumes inflation will average 3%, and that he can earn an 8% compound annual rate of return on his investments. How much does Jacob need to invest today in order to meet his goal?

    A. $260,056.99
    B. $272,681.46
    C. $274.369.28
    D. $290,182.38

54. According to the Principle of _____, a CFP® Board designee who has knowledge that another CFP® Board designee has committed a violation of the Code of Ethics which raises substantial questions as to the designee's honesty, trustworthiness or fitness as a CFP® Board designee in other respects, shall promptly inform the CFP® Board.

    A. Integrity
    B. Competence
    C. Professionalism
    D. Diligence

55. Lauren invests $4,000 into her **SEP IRA**. Each year, for the next 10 years, she is able to invest an additional $2,000. What is the value of Lauren's account at the end of 10 years if her investments earn 8% annually?

A. $20,337.42
B. $22,655.27
C. $37,608.82
D. $39,926.67

56. Mary wants to start her own business in 5 years. She needs to accumulate $200,000 in today's dollars to fund the start-up costs. She assumes inflation will average 4%, and that she can earn an 8% compound annual rate of return on her investments. What serial payment should Mary invest at the end of the first year to achieve her goal?

A. $31,284.18
B. $34,190.28
C. $37,039.13
D. $38,520.69

57. What is the **IRR** of a zero-coupon bond with a $1,000 face value, a current market price of $810, and 4 years until maturity?

A. 2.67%
B. 5.34%
C. 5.41%
D. 10.80%

58. If an **RIA** has up to _____ of assets under management, the **RIA** must register with the individual state(s) where the **RIA** maintains clients.

A. $15 million
B. $20 million
C. $25 million
D. $30 million

59. According to the Principle of _____, a CFP® Board designee shall make and/or implement only recommendations which are suitable for the client.

A. Competence
B. Diligence
C. Objectivity
D. Fairness

60. An individual who meets which of the following criteria must register as an investment advisor?

(1) The individual provides advice or analyses concerning securities.
(2) The individual is in the business of providing investment advice.
(3) The individual is a **CPA** or attorney whose investment advice is only incidental to his or her other activities.
(4) The individual provides investment advice for compensation.

A. (3) only
B. (1), (2), and (3) only
C. (1), (2), and (4) only
D. (2), (3), and (4) only

61. An advisor can satisfy the "brochure rule" by providing the client which of the following?

A. Form ADV, Part I
B. Form ADV, Part II
C. Client Service Agreement
D. Addendum of Trust

62. If an **RIA** has between _____ and _____ of assets under management, the **RIA** may register with either the applicable state(s) where the **RIA** maintains clients, or the **SEC** at the **RIA**'s discretion.

A. $20 million, $25 million
B. $25 million, $30 million
C. $30 million, $35 million
D. $35 million, $50 million

63. According to the Principle of _____, a **CFP®** Board designee shall enter into a financial planning engagement only when the relationship is warranted based on the individual's needs and objectives.

   A. Integrity
   B. Fairness
   C. Competence
   D. Diligence

64. Murray deposited $325 into his money market account at the end of each month for the past 3 years. His account is now worth $12,875. If interest was compounded monthly, what was the average annual compound rate of return Murray earned over the 3-year period?

   A. 6.5%
   B. 6.9%
   C. 7.3%
   D. 7.8%

For questions 65-74, match the consumer protection act with the description that follows. Use only one answer per blank. Answers may be used more than once or not at all.

   A. Fair Credit Reporting Act
   B. Truth in Lending Act

65. _____ The consumer must be told if information in his credit report has been used against him.

66. _____ The lender must inform the borrower of the annual interest rate being charged on a loan.

67. _____ The consumer has a right to know what is in his credit report.

68. _____ The consumer has a right to ask for his credit score.

69. _____ The cost of any credit life insurance must be disclosed to the borrower.

70. _____ The consumer has the right to dispute incomplete or inaccurate information in his credit report.

71. ____ Prepayment penalties must be disclosed to the borrower.

72. ____ Credit reporting agencies must correct or delete inaccurate, incomplete, or unverifiable information.

73. ____ A right of rescission clause must be included in a loan contract allowing the borrower three business days to nullify the contract.

74. ____ If a credit card is lost or stolen, the consumer is liable for a maximum loss of $50 per credit card.

75. Paula wants to save $40,000 for a down payment on a new motor home in 3 years. She can invest $1,000 at the beginning of each month, and she expects to earn 10% compounded monthly on her investments. How much will Paula have saved in 3 years? Will Paula be able to achieve her goal?

A. $40,278.48, No
B. $41,781.57, No
C. $42,130.00, Yes
D. $43,182.37, Yes

76. According to the Principle of _____, a CFP® Board designee shall use the CFP® marks in compliance with the rules and regulations of the CFP® Board.

A. Professionalism
B. Objectivity
C. Diligence
D. Confidentiality

77. Beth wants to give her nephew $15,000 to take a trip around the world in 8 years. How much should she invest today at an annual rate of 5% compounded annually to have $15,000 in 8 years?

A. $10,152.59
B. $11,330.64
C. $13,913.55
D. $15,070.89

78. Which of the following are among the economic goals of the Federal Reserve and the US Treasury?

(1) Full employment
(2) Stable prices
(3) Economic growth
(4) Decrease government spending

A. (1) and (4) only
B. (3) and (4) only
C. (1), (2), and (3) only
D. All of the above

79. Monetary policy refers to actions taken by the _____ to control the money supply, often by targeting a specific rate of interest.

A. US Treasury
B. Federal Reserve
C. Executive branch
D. US Secretary of the Treasury

80. Monetary policy is carried out through all but which of the following methods?

A. Taxation
B. Open market operations
C. Changing the reserve requirements
D. Changing the discount rate

81. What is the intrinsic value of a bond with a $1,000 face value, an 8% coupon, and 4 years until maturity? Comparable bonds are currently yielding 9.8%.

A. $941.60
B. $970.17
C. $1,000.00
D. $1,138.19

82. Which of the following describes actions taken by the Federal Reserve and their effect on the money supply?

(1) If the Federal Reserve sells government securities, it receives money in return, which increases the money supply.
(2) If the Federal Reserve sells government securities, it is considered contractionary policy.

A. (1) only
B. (2) only
C. None of the above
D. All of the above

For questions 83-86, match the stage of the business cycle with the description that follows. Use only one answer per blank. Answers may be used more than once or not at all.

A. Trough
B. Expansion
C. Contraction
D. Peak

83. _____ Recession

84. _____ Utilization at its lowest level

85. _____ Recovery

86. _____ GDP at its highest point

87. Pete would like to save $80,000 for his son's college education. His son will begin college in 13 years. Assume Pete can invest $10,000 now, and $600 at the end of each 3-month period. What annual rate of return is required for Pete to achieve his goal?

A. 1.90%
B. 1.93%
C. 7.59%
D. 7.73%

88. A recession is a decline in real **GDP** for _____ or more consecutive quarters. **A** depression is a decline in real **GDP** for _____ or more consecutive quarters.

A. 2, 4
B. 3, 6
C. 2, 6
D. 4, 6

89. Gross Domestic Product (**GDP**) = C + I + G + E. The variables C, I, G, and E stand for which of the following?

(1) C = Personal consumption
(2) I = Issuance of government bonds
(3) G = Government consumption
(4) E = Net exports

A. (1) and (3) only
B. (1) and (4) only
C. (2) and (4) only
D. (3) and (4) only

90. A **CFP®** practitioner is required to have _____ continuing education (**CE**) hours per reporting period in order to renew her certification.

A. 20
B. 25
C. 30
D. 40

91. Which of the following is the first step of the budgeting process?

A. List all categories and amounts of discretionary expenses.
B. Estimate all income and sources of income.
C. Determine how much needs to be saved.
D. List all categories and amounts of fixed expenses.

92. Which of the following is/are correct regarding the Code of Ethics?

   (1) The Code of Ethics describes the standards of ethical and professionally responsible conduct expected of CFP® Board designees.
   (2) The Code of Ethics attempts to define the standards of professional conduct of CFP® Board designees for the purposes of civil liability.

   A. (1) only
   B. (2) only
   C. None of the above
   D. All of the above

93. What is the IRR of a 1-year investment in a REIT, if $100 is invested at the beginning of each month? Assume the REIT's end of year value is $1,300.

   A. 7.35%
   B. 14.70%
   C. 17.32%
   D. 20.10%

94. Which of the following will result if money distributed from a 529 Plan is not used to pay for qualifying education expenses?

   A. Gains are taxed at capital gains rates, and a 10% penalty is applied.
   B. Gains are taxed as ordinary income, and a 10% penalty is applied.
   C. Gains are taxed at capital gains rates, and a 20% penalty is applied.
   D. Gains are taxed as ordinary income, and a 20% penalty is applied.

95. Which of the following are qualified expenses to be paid from a Coverdell Education Savings Account (ESA)?

(1) Computers and laptops
(2) Transportation
(3) Books and supplies
(4) Tuition, room, and board

A. (3) and (4) only
B. (1), (2), and (4) only
C. (2), (3), and (4) only
D. All of the above

96. The Code of Ethics consists of two parts: Part I – _____, and Part II – _____.

A. Rules, Principles
B. Rules, Ethics
C. Principles, Rules
D. Principles, Ethics

97. According to the Principle of _____, a CFP® Board designee shall satisfy all minimum continuing education requirements established by the CFP® Board.

A. Diligence
B. Competence
C. Professionalism
D. Integrity

98. Jon invested $10,000 in a high-yield money market account earning a 7% annual rate of return compounded monthly. What will be the value of Jon's account at the end of 9 years?

A. $15,301.43
B. $16,692.90
C. $17,389.48
D. $18,741.77

99. Nick has a balloon payment of $50,000 due in 6 years. If he can make a lump-sum payment today, how much should he offer to satisfy the loan if it is discounted at a rate of 8% compounded semiannually?

A. $31,029.49
B. $31,229.85
C. $31,398.30
D. $31,640.38

100. Which of the following is/are correct regarding income elasticity?

(1) An inferior product, such as margarine, has negative income elasticity.
(2) If a product has positive income elasticity, as income increases the quantity demanded decreases.

A. (1) only
B. (2) only
C. None of the above
D. All of the above

ANSWER KEY

1. B
The six steps of the financial planning process are:
(1) Establish the client-planner relationship.
(2) Gather data and determine goals and expectations.
(3) Analyze and evaluate the client's financial status.
(4) Develop and present the financial plan.
(5) Implement the financial plan.
(6) Monitor the financial plan.

The six steps of the financial planning process form the acronym "EGADIM".

2. C
According to the Principle of Integrity, a CFP® Board designee shall not solicit clients through false or misleading communications or advertisements.

3. D
If grounds for discipline have been established against a CFP® Board designee, the Disciplinary and Ethics Commission may impose any of the following forms of discipline. In level of severity they are:
(1) Require additional continuing education hours in any subject matter areas separate from, or in addition to, any form of discipline.
(2) Issue a private censure by letter of reprimand.
(3) Issue a public letter of admonition.
(4) Suspend the designee's right to use the CFP® mark for a specified period of time, not to exceed five years.
(5) Permanently revoke the designee's right to use the CFP® mark.

4. C
If an RIA has more than $30 million of assets under management, the RIA must register with the SEC.

5. C
Begin Mode
PMT = $1,400
n = 6 x 2 = 12
i = 12 / 2 = 6
FV = 0
PV = ? = $12,441.62

6. D
According to the Principle of Confidentiality, a CFP® Board designee shall treat client information as confidential except as required in response to proper legal process; as needed to establish an advisory or brokerage account; to defend against charges of wrongdoing; or in connection with a civil dispute between the CFP® Board designee and the client.

7. B
Establishing the client-planner relationship includes identifying the services to be provided; establishing the duration of the engagement; disclosing the method of compensation; and determining the roles and responsibilities of the client and financial planner.

8. B
PMT = -$2,000
n = 11
i = 8
PV = 0
FV = ? = $33,290.97

9. C
David's loss is limited to $50 per credit card. However, one card has only $30 charged against it, so his loss is limited to $30 for that card.

10. A
According to the Principle of Integrity, a CFP® Board designee shall not commingle client funds or other property with a CFP® Board designee's personal funds and/or other property of a CFP® Board designee's firm.

11. A
PV = -$910
n = 6 x 2 = 12
PMT = $1,000 x 0.11 = $110. $110 / 2 = $55
FV = $1,000
i = ? = 6.6097 x 2 = 13.22

12. B

Consumer debt payments, such as credit cards and vehicle loans, should not exceed 20% of net income.

13. C

Housing debt costs, including principal, interest, taxes, and insurance, should not exceed 28% of gross income.

14. C

Total debt payment should not exceed 36% of gross income.

15. D

Qualified expenses to be paid from a 529 plan include books, tuition, supplies, and room and board.

16. A

Coverdell Education Savings Accounts (ESAs) have a maximum contribution limit of $2,000 per beneficiary per year.

17. B

Contractionary policy is characterized by taxes increasing, public spending decreasing, and government borrowing decreasing.

18. A

Expansionary policy is characterized by taxes decreasing, public spending increasing, and government borrowing increasing.

19. B

Contractionary policy is characterized by taxes increasing, public spending decreasing, and government borrowing decreasing.

20. B

Both full-time and part-time students are eligible to receive Pell Grants. They are available to undergraduate students only and are distributed on the basis of financial need.

21. A

PV = -$600

n = 5

i = 9

PMT = 0

FV = ? = $923.17

22. C
Federal Supplemental Educational Opportunity Grants (SEOGs) are available to both part-time and full-time students.

23. B
Stafford Loans are administered by the Federal Family Education Loan Program (FFELP).

24. B
Perkins loans are available to both undergraduate and graduate students.

25. A
Parent Loans to Undergraduate Students (PLUS) are available to full-time students only.

26. B
The demand curve slopes down and to the right, indicating that as price decreases, the quantity demanded increases.

27. A
When a small change in price causes a large change in the quantity purchased, the product is considered to be elastic. This is common with products that have many available substitutes.

28. C
FV = $1,000
n = 5 x 2 = 10
i = 8.46 / 2 = 4.23
PMT = 0
PV = ? = $660.80

29. A
Inelastic goods have few available substitutes.

30. B
Perfect elasticity results in a horizontal demand curve. Perfect inelasticity results in a vertical demand curve.

31. C
FV = $1,000
n = 8 x 2 = 16
i = 12.6 / 2 = 6.3
PMT = $1000 x 0.10 = $100. $100 / 2 = $50
PV = ? = $871.29

32. D
Money in a Coverdell Education Savings Account (ESA) must be used by the time the beneficiary is 30 years of age.

33. C
According to the Second Law of Demand, when the price of a product increases, consumers will reduce their consumption more in the long run than in the short run. Thus, the demand for products is more elastic in the long run than in the short run.

34. C
PV = -30,000
n = 4
i = 12
PMT = 0
FV = ? = $47,205.58

35. D
A shift in the demand curve is caused by changes in consumer income; changes in the price of complement and substitute goods; changes in consumer expectations; and changes in consumer tastes and preferences.

36. C
A change in quantity supplied is identified as movement along the supply curve. It is the willingness of producers to offer the same product at different prices.

37. A
A change in consumer sentiment is a leading economic indicator.

38. B
The average prime rate charged by banks is a lagging economic indicator.

39. B
A change in the Consumer Price Index (CPI) is a lagging economic indicator.

40. A
Orders for durable goods are a leading economic indicator.

41. B
The average duration of unemployment is a lagging economic indicator.

42. A
A change in the money supply is a leading economic indicator.

43. A

Housing starts are a leading economic indicator.

44. A

According to the Principle of Fairness, a CFP® Board designee shall disclose conflicts of interest and sources of compensation.

45. C

A donor may contribute a total of five gift tax annual exclusion amounts on a one-time basis every five years to a 529 plan. $5 \times \$13,000 = \$65,000$.

46. A

FV = $95,000

n = 7.5 x 4 = 30

i = 9.5 / 4 = 2.375

PMT = 0

PV = ? = $46,979.26

47. D

A shift in the supply curve is caused by changes in resource prices, changes in technology, natural disasters, and political disruptions.

48. B

PMT = -$2,000

n = 5 x 2 = 10

i = 7 / 2 = 3.5

FV = 0

PV = ? = $16,633.21

49. C

The Principles of the Code of Ethics in the correct order are:

Principle 1: Integrity

Principle 2: Objectivity

Principle 3: Competence

Principle 4: Fairness

Principle 5: Confidentiality

Principle 6: Professionalism

Principle 7: Diligence

The seven principles form the acronym "IOCFCPD". Remember the phrase "Ideas Only Come From Careful Planning Daily".

50.A
FV = $150,000
n = 7 x 4 = 28
i = 10 / 4 = 2.5
PMT = 0
PV = ? = $75,131.67

51.B
To establish a Coverdell Education Savings Account (ESA), the beneficiary must be under age 18 unless the individual is designated as a special needs beneficiary.

52.C
PMT = -$2,000
n = 7 x 2 = 14
i = 6 / 2 = 3
PV = 0
FV = ? = $34,172.65

53.B
Begin Mode
PMT = $40,000
n = 8
i = [(1.08 / 1.03) − 1] x 100 = 4.8544
FV = 0
PV = ? = $272,681.46

54.C
According to the Principle of Professionalism, a CFP® Board designee who has knowledge that another CFP® Board designee has committed a violation of the Code of Ethics which raises substantial questions as to the designee's honesty, trustworthiness or fitness as a CFP® Board designee in other respects, shall promptly inform the CFP® Board.

55.C
PV = -$4,000
n = 10
i = 8
PMT = -$2,000
FV = ? = $37,608.82

56. D
FV = $200,000
n = 5
i = [(1.08 / 1.04) − 1] × 100 = 3.8462
PV = 0
PMT = ? = $37,039.13 × 1.04 = $38,520.69

57. B
PV = -$810
n = 4 x 2 = 8
FV = $1,000
PMT = 0
i = ? = 2.6690 x 2 = 5.34

58. C
If an RIA has up to $25 million of assets under management, the RIA must register with the individual state(s) where the RIA maintains clients.

59. B
According to the Principle of Diligence, a CFP® Board designee shall make and/or implement only recommendations which are suitable for the client.

60. C
An individual who meets the following criteria must register as an investment advisor:
(1) The individual provides advice or analyses concerning securities.
(2) The individual is in the business of providing investment advice.
(3) The individual provides investment advice for compensation.

61. B
There are two ways an advisor can satisfy the brochure rule:
(1) The advisor can provide the client with Form ADV, Part II.
(2) The advisor can provide an actual brochure that contains the same information that would be found in Form ADV, Part II.

62. B
If an RIA has between $25 million and $30 million of assets under management, the RIA may register with either the applicable state(s) where the RIA maintains clients, or the SEC at the RIA's discretion.

63. D
According to the Principle of Diligence, a CFP® Board designee shall enter into a financial planning engagement only when the relationship is warranted based on the individual's needs and objectives.

64. A

PMT = -$325

n = 3 x 12 = 36

FV = $12,875

PV = 0

i = ? = 0.5394 x 12 = 6.5

65. A

According to the Fair Credit Reporting Act, a consumer must be told if information in his credit report has been used against him.

66. B

According to the Truth in Lending Act, the lender must inform the borrower of the annual interest rate being charged on a loan.

67. A

According to the Fair Credit Reporting Act, a consumer has the right to know what is in his credit report.

68. A

According to the Fair Credit Reporting Act, a consumer has the right to ask for his credit score.

69. B

According to the Truth in Lending Act, the cost of any credit life insurance must be disclosed to the borrower.

70. A

According to the Fair Credit Reporting Act, a consumer has the right to dispute incomplete or inaccurate information in his credit report.

71. B

According to the Truth in Lending Act, prepayment penalties must be disclosed to the borrower.

72. A

According to the Fair Credit Report Act, credit reporting agencies must correct or delete inaccurate, incomplete, or unverifiable information.

73. B

According to the Truth in Lending Act, a right of rescission clause must be included in a loan contract allowing the borrower three business days to nullify the contract.

74. B
According to the Truth in Lending Act, if a credit card is lost or stolen, the consumer is liable for a maximum loss of $50 per credit card.

75. C
Begin Mode
PMT = -$1,000
n = 3 x 12 = 36
i = 10 / 12 = 0.8333
PV = 0
FV = ? = $42,130.00

Yes, Paula can achieve her goal because she will have more than $40,000.

76. A
According to the Principle of Professionalism, a CFP® Board designee shall use the CFP® marks in compliance with the rules and regulations of the CFP® Board.

77. A
FV = $15,000
n = 8
i = 5
PMT = 0
PV = ? = $10,152.59

78. C
The goals of the Federal Reserve and US Treasury are full employment, stable prices, and economic growth.

79. B
Monetary policy refers to actions taken by the Federal Reserve to control the money supply, often by targeting a specific rate of interest.

80. A
Monetary policy is carried out through open market operations, changing the reserve requirements, and changing the discount rate.

81. A
FV = $1,000
i = 9.8 / 2 = 4.9
n = 4 x 2 = 8
PMT = $1,000 x 0.08 = $80. $80 / 2 = $40
PV = ? = $941.60

82. B
If the Federal Reserve sells government securities, it receives money in return, which reduces the money supply. This is considered contractionary policy.

83. C
The contraction stage of the business cycle is characterized by recession.

84. A
At the trough of the business cycle, utilization will be at its lowest level.

85. B
The expansion stage of the business cycle is characterized by recovery.

86. D
At the peak of the business cycle, GDP will be at its highest point.

87. D
PV = -$10,000
n = 13 x 4 = 52
PMT = -$600
FV = $80,000
i = ? = 1.9322 x 4 = 7.73

88. C
A recession is a decline in real GDP for 2 or more consecutive quarters. A depression is a decline in real GDP for 6 or more consecutive quarters.

89. B
Gross Domestic Product (GDP) = C + I + G + E
C = Personal consumption
I = Gross private domestic investment
G = Government spending
E = Net exports

90. C
A CFP® practitioner is required to have 30 continuing education (CE) hours per reporting period in order to renew her certification.

91. B
The first step of the budgeting process is to estimate all income and sources of income. The next step is to review all fixed and discretionary expenses before determining how much will be saved or invested.

92. A
The Code of Ethics describes the standards of ethical and professionally responsible conduct expected of CFP® Board designees. It does not attempt to define the standards of professional conduct of CFP® Board designees for the purposes of civil liability.

93. B
Begin Mode
FV = $1,300
n = 1 x 12 = 12
PMT = -$100
PV = 0
i = ? = 1.2253 x 12 = 14.70

94. B
If money distributed from a 529 plan is not used to pay for qualifying education expenses, the gain is taxed as ordinary income and a 10% penalty is applied.

95. D
Qualified expenses to be paid from a Coverdell Education Savings Account (ESA) include computers and laptops, transportation, books and supplies, room and board, and tuition.

96. C
The Code of Ethics consists of two parts: Part I – Principles, and Part II – Rules.

97. B
According to the Principle of Competence, a CFP® Board designee shall satisfy all minimum continuing education requirements established by the CFP® Board.

98. D

PV = -$10,000

n = 9 x 12 = 108

i = 7 / 12 = 0.5833

PMT = 0

FV = ? = $18,741.77

99. B

FV = -$50,000

n = 6 x 2 = 12

i = 8 / 2 = 4

PMT = 0

PV = ? = $31,229.85

100. A

An inferior product, such as margarine, has negative income elasticity. If a product has positive income elasticity, as income increases the quantity demanded increases.

INSURANCE

QUESTIONS

1. **Which of the following is/are correct regarding the regulation of insurance companies and broker-dealers?**

   (1) Insurance company regulation occurs primarily at the state level.
   (2) Broker-dealer regulation occurs primarily at the state level.

   A. (1) only
   B. (2) only
   C. None of the above
   D. All of the above

2. **Enforceable contracts must have which of the following characteristics?**

   (1) Legally competent parties
   (2) Legal purpose
   (3) Consideration
   (4) Offer and acceptance

   A. (3) and (4) only
   B. (1), (2), and (4) only
   C. (1), (3), and (4) only
   D. All of the above

3. **All but which of the following are correct regarding torts?**

   A. A tort can be either civil or criminal in nature.
   B. The most common type of unintentional tort is negligence.
   C. A tort is a civil wrong.
   D. The most common type of intentional tort is assault and battery.

4. An agent is responsible to his or her _____, not to the _____.

    A. principal, company
    B. principal, client
    C. company, principal
    D. client, principal

For questions 5-7, match the term with the description that follows. Use only one answer per blank. Answers may be used more than once or not at all.

    A. Risk
    B. Peril
    C. Hazard

5. ____ An event that causes a loss, such as fire, lightening, smoke, or theft.

6. ____ The possibility of an adverse deviation from an expected outcome.

7. ____ A condition that increases the chance that a loss will occur.

8. According to the concept of adverse selection, individuals who are _____ likely to need insurance benefits are the ones _____ likely to purchase coverage.

    A. least, most
    B. most, least
    C. least, least
    D. most, most

9. Which of the following are required elements for a risk to be insurable?

(1) There must be a sufficient number of homogenous events to make the loss reasonably predictable.
(2) The loss must be definite and measurable.
(3) The loss must be catastrophic.
(4) The loss must be fortuitous or accidental.

A. (1) and (2) only
B. (1), (2), and (4) only
C. (2), (3), and (4) only
D. All of the above

For questions 10-13, match the method of risk management with the description that follows. Use only one answer per blank. Answers may be used more than once or not at all.

A. Avoid the risk
B. Transfer the risk
C. Reduce the risk
D. Retain the risk

10. _____ Low severity of loss + High probability of loss

11. _____ High severity of loss + High probability of loss

12. _____ Low severity of loss + Low probability of loss

13. _____ High severity of loss + Low probability of loss

14. According to the principal of _____, an insured will only be reimbursed for the amount of his or her actual loss, and cannot make a profit from the loss.

A. adhesion
B. waiver and estoppel
C. indemnity
D. rescission

15. When must an insurable interest exist for property and casualty insurance?

A. Only at the time the policy is written
B. Only at the time the loss is claimed
C. At the time the policy is written and at the time the loss is claimed
D. An insurable interest is required for life insurance only.

16. According to the reinstatement clause, an owner of a life insurance policy can reinstate his or her policy if all but which of the following occur?

A. An insurable interest still exists
B. The insured is still insurable
C. The policy lapsed due to non-payment of premium
D. The policy was surrendered for its cash value

17. Insurance contracts implement the _____ rule, which states that damages assessed against a negligent party should not be reduced simply because the injured party has insurance protecting against the specific peril.

A. parol evidence
B. collateral source
C. rescission
D. subrogation

For questions 18-21, match the term with the description that follows. Use only one answer per blank. Answers may be used more than once or not at all.

A. Negligence
B. Libel
C. Slander
D. Malpractice
E. Errors and omissions

18. _____ While playing baseball with friends, Garrett hit a foul ball through his neighbor's window. What may Garrett be guilty of?

19. ____ Mark was frustrated with the general contractor working on his new home and made unfounded accusations about the contractor in an email to neighbors. Mark may be found liable for damaging the contractor's reputation because he has committed what?

20. ____ Richard, a pharmacist, accidentally dispensed the wrong dosage of medication to a patient. What may Richard be guilty of?

21. ____ At a political rally the incumbent knowingly made false accusations about his opponent's criminal history. The incumbent's comments negatively affected how people thought of his opponent. The incumbent may be found liable for damages because he has committed what?

22. Tom's home would cost $200,000 to rebuild if it were destroyed. Insurance on the home is currently $120,000 with a $500 deductible. If a kitchen fire causes $30,000 of damage and Tom files a claim, how much will the insurance company pay?

A. $500
B. $22,000
C. $29,500
D. $30,000

23. Which of the following cannot be insured?

A. Commercial real estate
B. Private residence
C. Raw land
D. All of the above can be insured.

24. Which of the following are common exclusions that apply to homeowners insurance policies?

(1) Water damage
(2) Power failure
(3) Hail
(4) War

A. (1) and (3) only
B. (1), (2), and (4) only
C. (2), (3), and (4) only
D. All of the above

25. Which of the following parts of a personal auto policy (PAP) are paired with the correct description?

(1) Part A: Liability Coverage
(2) Part E: General Provisions
(3) Part C: Uninsured Motorist Coverage
(4) Part F: Duties after an Accident or Loss

A. (1) and (3) only
B. (2) and (4) only
C. None of the above
D. All of the above

26. All but which of the following are correct regarding umbrella insurance policies?

A. Policies often have a $1 million minimum amount of coverage.
B. Umbrella insurance is referred to as "excess liability coverage".
C. Umbrella insurance picks up where underlying coverages, such as life and disability insurance, leave off.
D. Policies can be purchased in increments of $1 million.

27. **Which of the following are characteristics of Preferred Provider Organization (PPO) plans?**

(1) The network selects a primary care physician for the patient.
(2) The physician is referred to as a "gate keeper" since he or she must recommend a patient for treatment by a specialist.
(3) PPOs contract with physicians and other providers who agree to take reduced fees in exchange for prompt payment and referrals.
(4) PPOs do not use a co-pay system.

A. (1) and (4) only
B. (2) and (3) only
C. (1), (2), and (3) only
D. (2), (3), and (4) only

28. **Medicare covers all but which of the following groups?**

A. Individuals age 65 or over
B. Those who have been receiving social security disability benefits for at least 12 months
C. Individuals who are on kidney dialysis treatment and are currently in end-stage renal failure
D. Those who are eligible for social security disability benefits and have ALS

29. **Which of the following is not one of the primary definitions of disability commonly found in disability income policies?**

A. Own occupation
B. Dual occupation
C. Modified own occupation
D. Any occupation

30. **Medicare Part A covers which of the following categories?**

(1) **Hospital care**
(2) **Skilled nursing care**
(3) **Home health care**
(4) **Diagnostic tests**

A. (1) and (2) only
B. (1) and (3) only
C. (1), (2), and (3) only
D. (2), (3), and (4) only

For questions 31-33, match the disability policy renewal provision with the description that follows. Use only one answer per blank. Answers may be used more than once or not at all.

A. Guaranteed renewable
B. Cancelable
C. Conditionally renewable
D. Noncancellable

31. ____ **The policy may not be canceled by the insurance company during the policy term, but the company may refuse to renew the policy for specific reasons listed in the contract.**

32. ____ **The premium schedule will never change unless the insured buys additional coverage in the future.**

33. ____ **The insured has the right to renew the policy for a stated number of years. Premiums cannot change unless the change is made for an entire class of policyholders.**

34. Which of the following is/are correct regarding long-term care insurance?

   (1) The amount of the deduction that may be claimed for long-term care premiums is limited to a dollar amount based on the individual's age.
   (2) Benefits paid to an insured from a long-term care policy are generally excluded from taxable income.

   A. (1) only
   B. (2) only
   C. None of the above
   D. All of the above

For questions 35-38, match the term with the description that follows. Use only one answer per blank. Answers may be used more than once or not at all.

   A. Adhesion
   B. Unilateral
   C. Aleatory
   D. Utmost good faith

35. _____ Insurance contracts are _____ contracts, meaning only the insurance company makes legally enforceable promises in the contract.

36. _____ Insurance contracts are contracts of _____, meaning an insured can only accept or reject an insurance contract and cannot modify its terms.

37. _____ According to the principle of _____, both parties to an insurance contract must disclose all facts truthfully or the contract may be reformed or rescinded.

38. _____ Insurance contracts are _____ contracts, meaning the amount of money exchanged between an insured and the insurance company is unequal.

39. If an insured selects a longer elimination period for a long-term care policy, the monthly premium will be _____ than if a shorter elimination period is selected.

   A. higher
   B. lower
   C. more expensive
   D. higher or lower

40. All but which of the following are characteristics of a life paid-up at 65 insurance policy?

A. It is a whole life policy with premiums increasing until they stop at age 65.
B. The policy will last beyond the insured's age 65.
C. The policy lapses at age 65 but may be renewed for longer.
D. The policy endows at age 100.

41. In an individual disability policy, premiums paid are _____ and benefits received in the event of disability are _____.

A. deductible, taxable
B. non-deductible, non-taxable
C. deductible, non-taxable
D. non-deductible, taxable

42. Which of the following are correct regarding universal life policies with the "Option A" death benefit?

(1) The death benefit includes the cash accumulation fund.
(2) The death benefit is equal to the face amount of the policy plus the accumulation fund.
(3) The mortality charges are based on the net amount at risk, which is the face amount of the policy minus the accumulation fund.
(4) The monthly mortality charges are based on the face amount of the policy every year.

A. (1) and (3) only
B. (1) and (4) only
C. (2) and (3) only
D. (2) and (4) only

43. A provision in a life insurance policy that prevents an insurer from revoking coverage because of alleged misstatements by an insured after a specified period, usually two years, is referred to as the _____.

A. indemnity clause
B. misstatement of age clause
C. statute of frauds clause
D. incontestable clause

44. The typical grace period for a life insurance policy is _____.

    A. 7 days
    B. 14 days
    C. 30 days
    D. 60 days

45. According to a typical suicide clause, if an insured commits suicide within the first two years after a life insurance policy is issued, which of the following will result?

    A. No death benefit will be paid.
    B. The full death benefit will be paid.
    C. The insurance company will pay only the cumulative premiums plus interest earned.
    D. The insurance company will pay only the cumulative premiums minus interest earned.

46. Which of the following are required to obtain a viatical settlement?

    (1) The insured must not be terminally ill.
    (2) The insured must have owned the policy for at least one year.
    (3) The current beneficiary of the policy must sign a release or waiver.
    (4) The insured must sign a release allowing the viatical settlement provider access to his or her medical records.

    A. (1) and (2) only
    B. (3) and (4) only
    C. (2), (3), and (4) only
    D. All of the above

47. If dividends distributed from a life insurance policy exceed the premiums paid to date, how are the dividends taxed?

    A. The dividends are taxed as ordinary income.
    B. The dividends are non-taxable because they are a return of premium.
    C. The dividends are taxed at long-term capital gains rates.
    D. The dividends are non-taxable until the policy is surrendered.

For questions 48-57, determine if the item listed is a life insurance non-forfeiture option, dividend option, or settlement option. Use only one answer per blank. Answers may be used more than once or not at all.

A. Non-forfeiture option
B. Dividend option
C. Settlement option

48. ____ Period certain and life

49. ____ Extended term

50. ____ Premium reduction

51. ____ Paid-up reduced amount

52. ____ Specified period

53. ____ Accumulate with interest

54. ____ Paid-up additions

55. ____ Pure life or single life

56. ____ Specified income

57. ____ One-year term

58. Partial loans and surrenders of MECs are taxed on a _____ basis. Partial loans and surrenders of non-MECs are taxed on a _____ basis.

A. FIFO, LIFO
B. LIFO, FIFO
C. LIFO, LIFO
D. FIFO, FIFO

59. How can a life insurance policy deemed to be a MEC be converted to a non-MEC?

A. Satisfy the guideline and premium corridor test
B. Satisfy the seven-pay test
C. Petition the IRS for a private letter ruling
D. Once a life insurance policy becomes a MEC, there is no way to reverse the tax treatment.

60. Which of the following are types of buy-sell agreements?

(1) Cross-purchase agreement
(2) Entity purchase agreement
(3) Cross-entity agreement
(4) Endorsement agreement

A. (1) and (2) only
B. (1) and (3) only
C. (2) and (3) only
D. (3) and (4) only

61. In a key-employee life insurance policy, life insurance is applied for, owned by, and payable to which of the following?

A. The insured
B. The insured's estate
C. The business
D. The insured's beneficiary

62. Which of the following methods can be used to calculate an individual's life insurance needs?

(1) Human life value method
(2) Needs analysis method

A. (1) only
B. (2) only
C. None of the above
D. All of the above

63. Which of the following are insurance industry rating services?

(1) A.M. Best
(2) Standard & Poor's
(3) NAIC
(4) Fitch

A. (1) and (2) only
B. (1), (2), and (4) only
C. (2), (3), and (4) only
D. All of the above

64. All but which of the following are correct regarding the process of underwriting an insurance policy?

A. Underwriting refers to the process of selecting, classifying, and pricing applicants for insurance.
B. Restrictive underwriting typically results in higher overall claims made by policyholders.
C. The underwriter is the individual who decides to accept or reject an application, and under what conditions the policy may be issued.
D. One of the objectives of underwriting is to generate revenue while at the same time limiting the insurance company's assumed risk.

65. Which of the following is not a type of annuity settlement option?

A. Single life
B. Installment refund
C. Life with period certain
D. Extended term

66. Which of the following is correct regarding covered perils in homeowners insurance policies?

A. The HO-2 form provides broad coverage on the dwelling and open coverage on personal property.
B. The HO-5 form provides open coverage on the dwelling and open coverage on personal property.
C. The HO-6 form is commonly used for condos and provides open coverage on the dwelling.
D. The HO-3 form provides broad coverage on the dwelling and broad coverage on personal property.

67. Which of the following is not a basic form of covered peril found in homeowners insurance policies?

A. Explosion
B. Smoke
C. Theft
D. Ruptured system

68. Annuity contracts issued after 8/13/82 are taxed on a _____ basis with interest taxed _____.

A. LIFO, last
B. LIFO, first
C. FIFO, last
D. FIFO, first

69. If an individual would like to protect herself not only against becoming totally disabled, but also against a reduction in income if she's forced to work fewer hours due to partial disability, which of the following provisions should be included in her disability policy?

A. Waiver of premium
B. Cost-of-living adjustment
C. Residual disability benefits
D. Change-of-occupation provision

70. A life insurance policy that pays a dividend is known as a _____.

A. non-participating policy
B. noncancellable policy
C. waiver of premium policy
D. participating policy

71.All but which of the following are characteristics of a modified endowment contract (MEC)?

A. The contract was entered into after 6/21/88.
B. The contract meets the requirements of a life insurance contract.
C. The contract meets the "seven-pay test".
D. The contract fails to meet the guideline premium and corridor test.

72. Which of the following statements accurately describes a typical whole life insurance policy?

(1) The premiums must be paid for the insured's entire lifetime, or for a period of at least ten years.
(2) The cash value cannot be used as collateral for a loan.
(3) The difference between a policy's face amount and the reserve must be greater than the cash surrender value at all times.
(4) The cash value must equal the face amount of coverage by the end of the mortality table.

A. (4) only
B. (2) and (3) only
C. (1), (2), and (3) only
D. All of the above

73. Long-term care policies have which of the following characteristics?

A. Coverage is usually not necessary because Medicare will provide adequate protection when an individual turns age 65.
B. Covered care can be provided only in a hospital or skilled nursing care facility.
C. Coverage must be provided for at least twelve months.
D. All of the above are correct.

74.All but which of the following are characteristics of universal life policies?

A. Unbundled structure
B. Flexible death benefit
C. Minimum guaranteed cash value
D. Flexible premium

75. Purchasing an insurance policy is suitable if potential losses have a _____ probability and _____ severity.

A. low, low
B. high, high
C. low, high
D. high, low

76. A waiver of premium clause:

A. waives the premium if additional insurance is purchased.
B. waives the premium in the event of disability.
C. waives the premium after a specific number of years.
D. waives the premium due to extreme financial hardship.

77. A variable life insurance policy will pay benefits that vary according to which of the following?

A. The flexibility of premiums paid
B. The variability of the mortality factor
C. The value of underlying investments
D. All of the above are correct.

78. Which of the following are criteria that should be evaluated when selecting an insurance company?

(1) The number of agents employed by the insurer
(2) The financial solvency of the insurer
(3) The services available to policyholders
(4) The claims settlement procedure of the insurer

A. (2) and (4) only
B. (1), (3), and (4) only
C. (2), (3), and (4) only
D. All of the above

79. Exaggerating a loss to an insurance company in order to collect a larger benefit payment is considered a _____ hazard.

A. moral
B. morale
C. physical
D. negligent

80. The proceeds from a life insurance policy will be included in the estate of an insured in which of the following circumstances?

(1) The proceeds from the policy are payable to the estate of the insured.
(2) The policy was transferred four years before death.
(3) The insured held incidents of ownership in the policy at the time of death.
(4) The proceeds from the policy are payable to an irrevocable life insurance trust.

A. (1) and (3) only
B. (1), (2), and (3) only
C. (2), (3), and (4) only
D. All of the above

81. Which one of the following describes speculative risk?

A. The risk that results from investment performance only.
B. The risk that results in an uncertain degree of gain or loss.
C. The risk that results in an opportunity to break even or achieve an uncertain degree of gain.
D. The risk that results in only an uncertain degree of loss.

82. After Paula (the insured) died, the insurance company discovered she was age 58, but according to her application she claimed she was age 56. Which of the following actions can the insurer take?

A. The insurer can deny paying the death benefit to Paula.
B. The insurer can cancel the policy if Paula died during the contestable period.
C. The insurer can decrease the face amount of the policy.
D. The insurer can force Paula to pay a higher premium.

83. The type of hazard that deals with negligence or carelessness is known as _____ hazard.

    A. moral
    B. morale
    C. physical
    D. negligent

84. Which of the following is/are correct regarding survivorship life insurance policies?

    (1) A survivorship life insurance policy results in a lower premium than a single life policy.
    (2) A survivorship life insurance policy can be used to fund the payment of estate taxes at the second spouse's death.

    A. (1) only
    B. (2) only
    C. None of the above
    D. All of the above

85. If an insured borrows a portion of the cash value from her whole life policy, which of the following is true?

    (1) The insured may borrow up to 100% of the face amount of the policy.
    (2) The loan must be repaid within five years.
    (3) The loan will not charge interest.
    (4) Any outstanding loans must be deducted from the face amount of the policy before death benefits are paid.

    A. (4) only
    B. (1) and (2) only
    C. (1), (2), and (4) only
    D. All of the above

86. Which of the following methods of valuing insured property does not take deprecia-tion into account?

A. Book value

B. Actual cash value

C. Replacement cost value

D. All of the above take depreciation into account.

87. All but which of the following are roles of the National Association of Insurance Com-missioners (NAIC)?

A. Suggest the drafting of insurance laws regulating insurance companies in their respective state.

B. Assist state insurance regulators in serving the public interest.

C. Pass legislation affecting insurance companies and their operations.

D. Regulate the conduct of insurance companies and agents in their respective state.

88. A small-business owner who maintains a retail store in a high-risk neighborhood installs shatterproof windows and a security system to prevent theft. Which method of risk management is the store owner using?

A. Avoidance

B. Diversification

C. Reduction

D. Transfer

89. Once an insurance contract is written and signed, any notes, comments, or other agreements that were discussed before the contract was signed are irrelevant accord-ing to which rule?

A. Collateral source rule

B. Utmost good faith rule

C. Parol evidence rule

D. Indemnity rule

90. An automatic premium loan provision may be available for which type of insurance policy?

    A. Term life insurance
    B. Disability insurance
    C. Permanent life insurance
    D. Long-term care insurance

91. A professional, such as a physician, who can cause bodily harm to another may require _____ insurance. A professional, such as a financial planner, who can cause monetary harm to another may require _____ insurance.

    A. malpractice, errors and omissions
    B. errors and omissions, malpractice
    C. malpractice, malpractice
    D. errors and omissions, errors and omissions

92. After a loss resulting from an automobile accident, the insured is expected to do which of the following?

    (1) Permit the insurer to gather medical reports and other relevant records.
    (2) Send the insurer notices and legal documents related to the claim.
    (3) Submit proof of loss when required by the insurer.
    (4) Submit to a physical exam at the insurer's request if it is relevant to the claim.

    A. (1) and (3) only
    B. (1), (2), and (3) only
    C. (2), (3), and (4) only
    D. All of the above

93. Which of the following parts of Medicare are paired with the correct description?

(1) Medicare Part A: Physician's insurance
(2) Medicare Part B: Hospital insurance
(3) Medicare Part C: Medicare Advantage
(4) Medicare Part D: Prescription drug coverage

A. (3) and (4) only
B. (1), (2), and (3) only
C. (1), (2), and (4) only
D. All of the above

94. Which definition of disability is most favorable to the insured and least desirable by the insurer?

A. Any occupation
B. Split definition
C. Modified own occupation
D. Own occupation

95. The activities of daily living (ADLs) which are used to measure the functional status of an individual include all but which of the following?

A. Dressing
B. Transferring
C. Walking
D. Toileting

96. Designating a life insurance policy's death benefit or cash surrender value to a creditor as security for a loan is referred to as _____.

A. absolute assignment
B. conditional assignment
C. collateral assignment
D. revocable assignment

97. Which of the following will result if the owner of a life insurance policy dies and the insured was someone other than the decedent?

A. The fair market value of the policy will be excluded from the decedent's gross estate.

B. The fair market value of the policy will be excluded from the decedent's gross estate, unless the policy is owned by an ILIT.

C. The fair market value of the policy will be included in the decedent's gross estate.

D. None of the above are correct.

98. If a company has three owners, how many life insurance policies must be purchased if an entity purchase buy-sell agreement is used?

A. 3

B. 6

C. 9

D. 12

99. Which of the following is a type of split-dollar life insurance policy in which the employee owns the death benefit and the employer pays the premium and owns the cash value?

A. Endorsement method

B. Employer loan method

C. Key-employee method

D. Collateral assignment method

100. Cameron, age 31, has a wife and three small children. He earns a high income as a dentist, but manages to save very little. He'd like to purchase a life insurance policy that will force him to save money and will last for his entire lifetime. Which type of insurance policy will meet Cameron's goals?

A. 10-year term

B. Second-to-die whole life

C. Whole life

D. Variable universal life

ANSWER KEY

1. A

Insurance company regulation occurs primarily at the state level. Broker-dealers are regulated at the federal level.

2. D

Enforceable contracts must have legally competent parties, a legal purpose, consideration, and offer and acceptance.

3. A

A tort is a civil wrong. It can be either intentional or unintentional in nature.

4. B

An agent is responsible to his or her principal, not to the client.

5. B

A peril is an event that causes a loss, such as fire, lightening, smoke, or theft.

6. A

Risk is the possibility of an adverse deviation from an expected outcome.

7. C

A hazard is a condition that increases the chance that a loss will occur.

8. D

According to the concept of adverse selection, individuals who are most likely to need insurance benefits are the ones most likely to purchase coverage.

9. B

The required elements for a risk to be insurable are:
(1) There must be a sufficient number of homogenous events to make the loss reasonably predictable.
(2) The loss must be definite and measurable.
(3) The loss must not be catastrophic.
(4) The loss must be fortuitous or accidental.

10. C
If there is a low severity and high probability of loss, the risk should be reduced.

11. A
If there is a high severity and high probability of loss, the risk should be avoided.

12. D
If there is a low severity and low probability of loss, the risk should be retained.

13. B
If there is a high severity and low probability of loss, the risk should be transferred.

14. C
According to the principal of indemnity, an insured will only be reimbursed for the amount of his or her actual loss, and cannot make a profit from the loss.

15. C
For property and casualty insurance to be underwritten, an insurable interest must exist at the time the policy is written and at the time the loss is claimed.

16. D
If a life insurance policy is surrendered for its cash value it may not be reinstated.

17. B
Insurance contracts implement the collateral source rule, which states that damages assessed against a negligent party should not be reduced simply because the injured party has insurance protecting against the specific peril.

18. A
Negligence

19. B
Libel

20. D
Malpractice

21. C
Slander

22. B
Step 1: 80% of $200,000 = $160,000
Step 2: $120,000 / $160,000 = 75%
Step 3: 75% of $30,000 = $22,500
Step 4: $22,500 - $500 = $22,000 paid by the insurance company

23. C
Raw land cannot be insured.

24. B
The common exclusions that apply to all forms of homeowners insurance policies are water damage, neglect, ordinance of law, earth movement, power failure, war, nuclear hazard, and intentional loss.

25. A
The six parts of the personal auto policy (PAP) are:
Part A: Liability Coverage
Part B: Medical Payments Coverage
Part C: Uninsured Motorist Coverage
Part D: Coverage for Damage to Your Auto
Part E: Duties after an Accident or Loss
Part F: General Provisions

26. C
Umbrella insurance picks up where underlying coverages, such as home and auto insurance, leave off.

27. B
In a PPO plan, the patient selects a primary care physician from a list of providers. PPOs use a co-pay system.

28. B
Medicare covers those who have been receiving social security disability benefits for at least 24 months.

29. B
The primary definitions of disability found in disability income policies are own occupation, modified own occupation, and any occupation.

30. C
Medicare Part A covers hospital care, skilled nursing care, home health care, and care in a hospice facility for the terminally ill.

31. C
A conditionally renewable policy may not be canceled by the insurance company during the policy term, but the company may refuse to renew the policy for specific reasons listed in the contract.

32. D
In a noncancellable policy, the premium schedule will never change unless the insured buys additional coverage in the future.

33. A
A guaranteed renewable policy gives the insured the right to renew the policy for a stated number of years. The insurer cannot change the premium unless the change is made for an entire class of policyholders.

34. D
The amount of the deduction that may be claimed for long-term care premiums is limited to a dollar amount based on the individual's age. Benefits paid to an insured from a long-term care policy are generally excluded from taxable income.

35. B
Insurance contracts are unilateral contracts, meaning only the insurance company makes legally enforceable promises in the contract.

36. A
Insurance contracts are contracts of adhesion, meaning an insured can only accept or reject an insurance contract and cannot modify its terms.

37. D
According to the principle of utmost good faith, both parties to an insurance contract must disclose all facts truthfully or the contract may be reformed or rescinded.

38. C
Insurance contracts are aleatory contracts, meaning the amount of money exchanged between an insured and the insurance company is unequal.

39. B
If an insured selects a longer elimination period for a long-term care policy, the monthly premium will be lower than if a shorter elimination period is selected.

40. C
A life paid-up at 65 policy is a whole life policy with premiums increasing so they stop at age 65, but the policy is guaranteed to last until, and endow, at age 100.

41. B

In an individual disability policy, premiums paid are non-deductible and benefits received in the event of disability are non-taxable.

42. A

With "Option A" universal life policies, the death benefit includes the cash accumulation fund. The mortality charges are based on the net amount at risk, which is the face amount of the policy minus the accumulation fund.

43. D

A provision in a life insurance policy that prevents an insurer from revoking coverage because of alleged misstatements by an insured after a specified period, usually two years, is referred to as the incontestable clause.

44. C

The typical grace period for a life insurance policy is 30 days.

45. C

In most states, if an insured commits suicide within the first two years after a policy is issued, the insurance company will pay only the cumulative premiums plus interest earned.

46. B

In order to obtain a viatical settlement, the insured must be terminally ill and must have owned the policy for at least two years. The current beneficiary of the policy must sign a release or waiver. The insured must sign a release allowing the viatical settlement provider access to his or her medical records.

47. A

If dividends distributed from a life insurance policy exceed the premiums paid to date, the dividends are taxed as ordinary income.

48. C

Period certain and life is a type of life insurance settlement option.

49. A

Extended term is a type of life insurance non-forfeiture option.

50. B

Premium reduction is a type of life insurance dividend option.

51. A

Paid-up reduced amount is a type of life insurance non-forfeiture option.

52. C

Specified period is a type of life insurance settlement option.

53. B

Accumulate with interest is a type of life insurance dividend option.

54. B

Paid-up additions is a type of life insurance dividend option.

55. C

Pure life or single life is a type of life insurance settlement option.

56. C

Specified income is a type of life insurance settlement option.

57. B

One-year term is a type of life insurance dividend option.

58. B

Partial loans and surrenders of MECs are taxed on a LIFO basis. Partial loans and surrenders of non-MECs are taxed on a FIFO basis.

59. D

Once a life insurance policy becomes a MEC, there is no way to reverse the tax treatment.

60. A

Cross-purchase agreements and entity purchase agreements are types of buy-sell agreements.

61. C

In a key-employee life insurance policy, life insurance is applied for, owned by, and payable to the business.

62. D

The human life value method and needs analysis method can be used to calculate an individual's life insurance needs.

63. B

The insurance industry rating services are A.M. Best, Standard & Poor's, Moody's, and Fitch.

64. B
Restrictive underwriting typically results in lower overall claims made by policyholders.

65. D
The annuity settlement options are cash, single life, life with period certain, joint-and-survivor, and installment refund.

66. B
The HO-5 form of homeowners insurance provides open coverage on the dwelling and open coverage on personal property.

67. D
Basic Form of covered perils: HARVEST WFL
Hail, aircraft, riot, vandalism, vehicles, volcanic eruption, explosion, smoke, theft, windstorm, fire, lightning

Broad Form of covered perils: Basic Form + FAR
Falling objects, freezing pipes, artificially generated electricity, ruptured system

68. B
Annuity contracts issued after 8/13/82 are taxed on a LIFO basis with interest taxed first.

69. C
Residual disability benefits cover partial disability.

70. D
A life insurance policy that pays a dividend is known as a participating policy.

71. C
A MEC is a life insurance contract that fails to meet the "seven-pay test".

72. A
The cash value of a whole life insurance policy must equal the face amount of coverage by the end of the mortality table.

73. C
Long-term care coverage must be provided for at least twelve months.

74. C
Universal life policies do not have a minimum guaranteed cash value.

75. C
Purchasing an insurance policy is suitable if potential losses have a low probability and high severity.

76. B
A waiver of premium clause waives the premium in the event of disability.

77. C
A variable life insurance policy will pay benefits that vary according to the value of the underlying investments.

78. C
When evaluating an insurance company, the important factors to consider are the financial solvency of the insurer, the services available to policyholders, and the claims settlement procedure of the insurer.

79. A
Exaggerating a loss to an insurance company in order to collect a larger benefit payment is considered a moral hazard.

80. A
The proceeds from a life insurance policy will be included in an insured's estate if the proceeds from the policy are payable to his or her estate, or if the insured held any incidents of ownership in the policy at the time of death.

81. B
Speculative risk results in an uncertain degree of gain or loss.

82. C
The insurance company can decrease the face amount of Paula's policy if she misstated her age on her application. The death benefit will be adjusted to what the premiums paid would have purchased if she had not misstated her age.

83. B
The type of hazard that deals with negligence or carelessness is known as morale hazard.

84. D
A survivorship life insurance policy results in a lower premium than a single life policy. The policy can be used to fund the payment of estate taxes at the second spouse's death.

85. A

Any outstanding policy loans must be deducted from the face amount of a life insurance policy before death benefits are paid.

86. C

A property's replacement cost value does not take depreciation into account.

87. C

The National Association of Insurance Commissioners (NAIC) does not pass legislation. That is the role of state legislatures.

88. C

The store owner is reducing the chance that vandalism or theft will occur by installing shatterproof windows and a security system.

89. C

According to the parol evidence rule, once an insurance contract is written and signed, any notes, comments, or other agreements that were discussed before the contract was signed are irrelevant.

90. C

An automatic premium loan provision may be available only for permanent forms of life insurance.

91. A

A professional, such as a physician, who can cause bodily harm to another, may require malpractice insurance. A professional, such as a financial planner, who can cause monetary harm to another, may require errors and omissions insurance.

92. D

After a loss resulting from an automobile accident, the insured is expected to permit the insurer to gather medical reports and other relevant records; send the insurer notices and legal documents related to the claim; submit proof of loss when required by the insurer; and submit to a physical exam at the insurer's request if it is relevant to the claim.

93. A

Medicare Part A: Hospital insurance
Medicare Part B: Physician's insurance
Medicare Part C: Medicare Advantage
Medicare Part D: Prescription drug coverage

94. D

The "own occupation" definition of disability is most favorable to the insured because it contains the broadest definition of disability.

95. C

The six activities of daily living (ADLs) are dressing, transferring, toileting, eating, bathing, and maintaining continence.

96. C

Designating a life insurance policy's death benefit or cash surrender value to a creditor as security for a loan is referred to as collateral assignment.

97. C

If the owner of a life insurance policy dies and the insured was someone other than the decedent, the fair market value of the policy will be included in the decedent's gross estate.

98. A

If a company has three owners, then three life insurance policies will be purchased (one for each owner) if an entity purchase buy-sell agreement is used.

99. A

The endorsement method of split-dollar life insurance is being characterized by the employee owning the death benefit, and the employer paying the premium and owning the cash value.

100. C

A whole life policy will force Cameron to pay premiums, act as a forced savings plan, and last for his entire lifetime.

TAX PLANNING

QUESTIONS

1. Which of the following are required to deduct alimony payments?

   (1) Payments must be made in cash.
   (2) Payments may extend beyond the death of the payee.
   (3) The payor and payee are permitted to live together.
   (4) Payments cannot stop upon the contingency of a child turning age 18.

   A. (1) and (3) only
   B. (1) and (4) only
   C. (1), (2), and (3) only
   D. (2), (3), and (4) only

2. For estimated tax payments, what is the penalty imposed on a self-employed taxpayer who did not have any income tax liability for the preceding year, but failed to withhold $10,000 in tax payments in the current year?

   A. $0 penalty
   B. $1,000 penalty
   C. $2,000 penalty
   D. The penalty depends on the individual's income tax bracket.

3. In order to deduct moving expenses, the distance between a taxpayer's new job and old residence must be at least _____ greater than the distance between the taxpayer's old job and old residence.

   A. 30 miles
   B. 50 miles
   C. 60 miles
   D. 100 miles

4. **Which of the following is correct regarding the amount of taxes withheld from an employee's paycheck based on the number of exemptions he or she claimed on IRS Form W-4?**

A. The more exemptions that are claimed, the less tax is withheld from an employee's paycheck.
B. The fewer exemptions that are claimed, the less tax is withheld from an employee's paycheck.
C. The number of exemptions claimed does not impact the tax withholding.
D. The relationship between the number of exemptions claimed and the taxes withheld cannot be determined from the information provided.

5. **Which of the following are considered secondary sources of tax information?**

(1) Periodicals
(2) Newsletters
(3) Books
(4) Articles

A. (1) and (2) only
B. (1), (3), and (4) only
C. None of the above
D. All of the above

For questions 6-13, match the tax penalty with the description that follows. Use only one answer per blank. Answers may be used more than once or not at all.

A. 20% of the deficiency
B. 75% of the deficiency
C. 5% penalty per month, up to a maximum of 25%
D. 0.5% penalty per month, up to a maximum of 25%
E. $500 penalty
F. $1,000 penalty

6. ____ **Failure to file a tax return**

7. ____ **Negligence**

8. ____ **Filing a frivolous tax return**

9. ____ **Civil fraud**

10. _____ Aiding and abetting a tax liability understatement

11. _____ Substantial understatement of tax liability

12. _____ The tax return has been filed, but taxes have not been paid

13. _____ Promoting abusive tax shelters

14. Which of the following are above-the-line deductions that may be claimed without a taxpayer itemizing deductions?

(1) Capital losses
(2) Deductible traditional IRA contributions
(3) Ordinary and necessary business (Schedule C) expenses
(4) Alimony paid

A. (1) and (3) only
B. (1), (2), and (3) only
C. (2), (3), and (4) only
D. All of the above

15. Which of the following is/are correct regarding tax credits?

(1) A refundable tax credit cannot reduce a taxpayer's income tax liability below zero.
(2) A non-refundable tax credit can reduce a taxpayer's income tax liability below zero.

A. (1) only
B. (2) only
C. None of the above
D. All of the above

16. To claim a dependency tax exemption, all but which of the following tests must be met?

A. Support test
B. Age test
C. Member of household test
D. Gross income test

17. **Which of the following professionals is not permitted to represent a taxpayer when audited by the IRS?**

    A. CPA
    B. Enrolled actuary
    C. CFP®
    D. Enrolled agent

18. **Which of the following is/are correct regarding the taxable wage base applied to social security and Medicare taxes paid by self-employed individuals?**

    (1) There is a taxable wage base applied to the social security portion of a self-employed individual's income, above which amount the 12.4% tax does not need to be paid.
    (2) There is no taxable wage base applied to the Medicare portion of a self-employed individual's income, and the 2.9% tax must always be paid.

    A. (1) only
    B. (2) only
    C. None of the above
    D. All of the above

19. **Kathy has self-employment income of $50,000 for the current year. How much self-employment tax must she pay?**

    A. $3,825
    B. $5,350
    C. $7,065
    D. $7,650

20. **According to the kiddie tax rules, if a child under the age of _____, or under the age of _____ if a full time student, has unearned income exceeding the annual threshold, the excess is taxed at the _____ marginal tax rate.**

    A. 18, 21, parent's
    B. 21, 24, parent's
    C. 19, 24, child's
    D. 19, 24, parent's

21. **If a taxpayer would like to change accounting methods, such as switching from the cash to accrual method of reporting income and expenses, which of the following must occur?**

   A. The taxpayer must receive approval from a CPA.
   B. The taxpayer must receive approval from the IRS.
   C. The taxpayer is not required to receive approval and can make the change at will.
   D. The taxpayer is not permitted to change the accounting method used.

22. **Which of the following is correct regarding long-term contracts?**

   A. The duties performed under the contract must be completed within ten years after the year in which construction begins.
   B. The duties performed under the contract must be completed within three years after the year in which construction begins.
   C. The duties performed under the contract must not be completed within the same year in which construction begins.
   D. The duties performed under the contract must not be completed within two years after the year in which construction begins.

23. **When gifts of property are claimed as income tax deductions in excess of _____, the donor must obtain a qualified appraisal for each item donated and must include a copy of the appraisal with the tax return.**

   A. $50
   B. $500
   C. $1,000
   D. $5,000

24. **Non-business bad debts are deductible as _____ on Schedule D of IRS Form 1040. The amount deductible is limited to the taxpayer's basis in the debt.**

   A. long-term capital losses
   B. short-term capital losses
   C. passive losses
   D. portfolio losses

25. **All but which of the following are characteristics of a sole proprietorship?**

    A. Simplest form of business entity
    B. No formal legal requirements
    C. Lack of continuity of business life
    D. Limited liability for the owner

26. **The amount of Section 1244 stock that can be deducted as an ordinary loss is limited to how much per year?**

    (1) $50,000 if single
    (2) $50,000 if filing a joint return
    (3) $100,000 if single
    (4) $100,000 if filing a joint return

    A. (1) and (3) only
    B. (1) and (4) only
    C. (2) and (3) only
    D. (2) and (4) only

27. **Which IRS tax form serves as an informational return used to report income, gains, losses, deductions, and credits from the operation of a partnership?**

    A. IRS Form 1065
    B. IRS Form 1060
    C. IRS Form 1040
    D. IRS Form 706

28. **Which of the following are among the requirements for a valid S Corp election?**

    (1) Only one class of stock permitted.
    (2) There may be no more than 75 shareholders.
    (3) It must be a domestic corporation.
    (4) Shareholders must be US citizens or residents.

    A. (1) and (3) only
    B. (1), (2), and (4) only
    C. (1), (3), and (4) only
    D. (2), (3), and (4) only

29. Any charitable contribution that is disallowed because of the limitation with respect to AGI can be carried forward for the lesser of _____ or death, and may be deducted on the donor's future income tax returns.

A. 3 years
B. 5 years
C. 10 years
D. 20 years

30. A C Corp may be subject to all but which of the following taxes?

A. Personal service corporation tax
B. Accumulated earnings tax
C. Accumulated holding company tax
D. Personal holding company tax

31. If payments to an ex-spouse terminate when a child turns age 18, rather than when the spouse remarries, which of the following will result?

A. The payments will be non-deductible to the payor and non-taxable to the payee. The payments will be considered child support.
B. The payments will be non-deductible to the payor and non-taxable to the payee. The payments will be considered alimony.
C. The payments will be deductible by the payor and taxable to the payee. The payments will be considered child support.
D. The payments will be deductible by the payor and taxable to the payee. The payments will be considered alimony.

32. How is the original basis of a newly acquired asset calculated? Assume the asset was acquired at an arm's length transaction from a non-related party.

A. Cost minus expenses of sale, such as sales tax paid, installation costs, freight charges, and commissions incurred in acquiring the asset
B. Cost plus expenses of sale, such as sales tax paid, installation costs, freight charges, and commissions incurred in acquiring the asset
C. Cost plus commissions incurred in acquiring the asset only
D. Cost minus commissions incurred in acquiring the asset only

33. What are the tax consequences if an installment sale occurs and the buyer is a family member who then sells the purchased property within two years after acquiring it?

    A. The family member who bought the property must recognize all gain deferred by the installment sale in the year of the subsequent sale.

    B. The original seller must recognize all gain deferred by the installment sale in the year of the subsequent sale.

    C. The new buyer (non-family member) must recognize all gain deferred by the installment sale in the year of the sale.

    D. There are no adverse tax consequences because the one-year holding period requirement has been satisfied.

For questions 34-36, match the cost recovery term with the description that follows. Use only one answer per blank. Answers may be used more than once or not at all.

    A. Amortization
    B. Depreciation
    C. Depletion

34. _____ The process by which the tax basis of natural resources is recovered.

35. _____ The process by which the tax basis of intangible assets is recovered.

36. _____ The process by which the tax basis of tangible assets is recovered.

37. In a like-kind exchange, a taxpayer has _____ days after the date the relinquished property is transferred to identify potential replacement properties. The exchange must be completed within _____ days after the transfer of the relinquished property.

    A. 30, 45
    B. 45, 90
    C. 45, 180
    D. 60, 90

38. To satisfy the ownership test for the Section 121 exclusion, the home must have been owned and used as a principal residence for at least _____ of the _____ years preceding the date of sale.

A. 1, 3
B. 1, 5
C. 2, 3
D. 2, 5

39. All but which of the following are characteristics of a C Corp?

A. Subject to double taxation
B. Perpetual life
C. Must have stock available for purchase on a stock exchange
D. Potential for classification as a personal service corporation (PSC)

40. *"A loss on the sale of property between related parties is disallowed for income tax purposes."* In this statement, "related parties" includes which of the following?

(1) Lineal descendants
(2) An individual and corporation if the individual owns more than 50% of the value of outstanding stock
(3) A grantor and trustee of a trust
(4) An executor and beneficiary of an estate

A. (1) and (2) only
B. (1), (3), and (4) only
C. (2), (3), and (4) only
D. All of the above

41. Which of the following are preference items or adjustments for AMT?

(1) The bargain element of nonqualified stock options
(2) General obligation municipal bonds
(3) Oil and gas percentage depletion
(4) Depreciation (ACRS and MACRS)

A. (1) and (2) only
B. (3) and (4) only
C. (1), (3), and (4) only
D. All of the above

For questions 42-48, match the type of charity with the description that follows. Use only one answer per blank. Answers may be used more than once or not at all.

A. Public charity
B. Private charity

42. _____ Government entities

43. _____ Churches and synagogues

44. _____ Fraternal organizations

45. _____ Educational organizations

46. _____ Veteran organizations

47. _____ Not-for-profit hospitals

48. _____ Private foundations

49. The holding period of property inherited from a decedent is considered to be _____ in nature.

A. sometimes short-term
B. always short-term
C. sometimes long-term
D. always long-term

50. Long-term capital gains tax rates apply if an asset is held for:

A. at least 12 months.
B. longer than 12 months.
C. at least 6 months using the half-year convention.
D. longer than 6 months using the half-year convention.

51. A closely held C Corp will be classified as a personal service corporation (PSC) if it falls under which of the following categories?

(1) Health (doctors and dentists)
(2) Engineering
(3) Accounting and architectural
(4) Law

A. (1) and (4) only
B. (1), (2), and (3) only
C. (2), (3), and (4) only
D. All of the above

52. Which of the following describes an itemized deduction?

A. A trade or business expense deductible from AGI
B. A personal expense deductible from AGI
C. A trade or business expense deductible in arriving at gross income
D. A personal expense deductible in arriving at gross income

53. A doctor starting a new medical practice is concerned about limiting her personal liability. She would like to have flow-through taxation and the ability to easily sell interests in her practice in the future. Which of the following entities is most suitable for the doctor to meet her goals?

A. S Corp
B. C Corp
C. Sole proprietorship
D. Limited partnership

54. Last year Jessica had an **AGI** of $115,000 and paid $28,000 in income taxes. She expects her tax liability this year to be $25,000. What is the minimum estimated tax payment Jessica must make in order to avoid the underpayment penalty?

A. $21,200
B. $22,500
C. $25,000
D. $28,000

55. Which of the following entities are subject to graduated corporate income tax rates?

(1) LLC
(2) S Corp
(3) C Corp
(4) Personal service corporation (PSC)

A. (3) only
B. (2) and (3) only
C. (1), (2), and (4) only
D. All of the above

56. Which of the following entities will protect owners from liability beyond the amount they personally invested?

(1) C Corp
(2) Limited partnership
(3) LLC
(4) S Corp

A. (1) and (4) only
B. (2) and (3) only
C. (1), (3), and (4) only
D. All of the above

57. Which of the following qualify as alimony?

A. Paying child support
B. Paying the payor spouse's mortgage (The payee lives in the house alone.)
C. Paying $5,000 to an ex-spouse's IRA
D. None of these qualify as alimony.

58. Two business associates, Carl and Mark, would like to enter into a like-kind exchange. Currently, Carl owns a rental property and Mark owns a home. Which of the following is correct regarding the exchange Carl and Mark are considering?

A. Both Carl and Mark are eligible to do a like-kind exchange, as long as the transferred properties will be used for rental purposes.
B. Carl can do a like-kind exchange if he uses the new property for rental purposes.
C. Mark can do a like-kind exchange if he uses the new property for rental purposes.
D. Neither Carl nor Mark are eligible to do a like-kind exchange because Mark owns a home.

59. Seth (AGI of $150,000) donated mutual funds to a local college with a fair market value of $85,000. He purchased the stock nine months ago for $80,000. What is Seth's maximum allowable charitable contribution for the current year?

A. $37,500
B. $75,000
C. $80,000
D. $95,000

60. Which of the following is/are correct regarding tax credits and deductions?

(1) A deduction is more beneficial to a higher-bracket taxpayer.
(2) A credit is more beneficial to a lower-bracket taxpayer.

A. (1) only
B. (2) only
C. None of the above
D. All of the above

61. Each year Chris rents out his beachfront home in Miami for 14 days. Because of his home's prime location, Chris is able to charge $5,000 per week. Which of the following is true?

A. Any repairs necessary would be deductible, but Chris is not permitted to show a loss.

B. Chris does not have to report the $5,000 income.

C. In addition to deducting repair costs, Chris can deduct a portion of his real estate taxes and depreciation.

D. Chris does not have to report the $10,000 income.

62. Stephanie teaches piano lessons at the local community center as an independent contractor. Which of the following taxes is Stephanie required to pay?

A. Income tax

B. Medicare payroll tax

C. Social security payroll tax

D. All of the above are correct.

63. Golf Solutions, an S Corp, was started five years ago for $55,000 cash. Due to unforeseen business problems, the owner had to lend the company another $30,000 to stay in operation. This year Golf Solutions has a net operating loss of $95,000. How much can the owner deduct as a loss on his tax return?

A. $30,000

B. $55,000

C. $85,000

D. $95,000

64. Tim purchased a painting for $9,000. Years later, when the painting was worth $5,000, he gave it to his brother, John, as a gift. Seven months later, John sold the painting for $3,000. Assuming John paid no gift taxes on the painting when he received it, what was John's net gain or loss on the sale?

A. $2,000 loss

B. $3,000 loss

C. $6,000 loss

D. No gain or loss will be recognized.

65. **Which of the following is correct regarding use of the home office deduction?**

A. The home office deduction can generate a loss to be used against income from a taxpayer's other activities.

B. The costs associated with running a home office can be deducted if the office is used primarily for business purposes.

C. In order to take the home office deduction, the office must be either the taxpayer's principal place of business, or where he or she meets with patients or clients in the normal course of business.

D. All of the above are correct.

66. **Which of the following are considered taxable income?**

(1) Workers compensation
(2) Child support
(3) Alimony
(4) Premiums paid by an employer on $75,000 of group term life insurance

A. (1) and (3) only
B. (3) and (4) only
C. (1), (3), and (4) only
D. All of the above

67. **A real estate developer sold a building to his church for $300,000. The fair market value of the building at the time of sale was $900,000. The seller's original basis in the land was $100,000. What is the taxable gain resulting from the sale?**

A. $0
B. $266,667
C. $333,333
D. $600,000

68. Which of the following miscellaneous itemized deductions are subject to the 2% of AGI floor?

(1) Work uniforms not suitable for regular wear
(2) Professional and business association dues
(3) Gambling losses to the extent of winnings
(4) Costs of looking for a new job

A. (1) and (4) only
B. (1), (2), and (3) only
C. (1), (2), and (4) only
D. (2), (3), and (4) only

69. When property is transferred for less than full consideration of money or money's worth, the value of the gift is equal to which of the following?

A. The value of the property transferred less the consideration received
B. The value of the property transferred plus the consideration received
C. The value of the consideration received
D. The lesser of the value of the property or the consideration received

70. The majority of individual tax returns filed in the US use the _____ method of accounting.

A. cash
B. accrual
C. hybrid
D. long-term contract

71. Mike has taxable income of $200,000 and a tax liability of $55,000. Mary has taxable income of $150,000 and a tax liability of $35,000. The tax rate structure being used to tax Mike and Mary is _____.

A. proportional
B. value added
C. progressive
D. flat

72. A taxpayer may petition for redetermination of an assessed income tax penalty and receive a jury trial in which of the following courts?

A. US Tax Court
B. US District Court
C. US Court of Appeals
D. US Appellate Court

73. Jim and Kate were married when Jim died unexpectedly on February 15 of the current year. They had no dependents. Which of the following is Kate's tax filing status for the current year?

A. Single
B. Married filing separately
C. Married filing jointly
D. Head of household

74. Which of the following is/are correct regarding capital losses?

(1) Capital losses have a two-year carry back period.
(2) Capital losses have a five-year carry forward period.

A. (1) only
B. (2) only
C. None of the above
D. All of the above

75. Which of the following represents the maximum amount of capital loss that a single taxpayer can deduct in a single year?

A. Up to the amount of capital gain
B. Up to the amount of capital gain plus $3,000
C. Up to the amount of capital gain plus $6,000
D. $3,000 only

76. A wash sale occurs when an investor acquires substantially identical stock during the _____ days prior to, or _____ days after the date of sale.

    A. 30, 30
    B. 45, 45
    C. 30, 45
    D. 45, 30

77. In calculating alternative minimum taxable income (AMTI), a taxpayer can deduct which of the following?

    (1) Qualified personal residence interest
    (2) Casualty losses in excess of 10% of AGI
    (3) Medical expenses in excess of 7.5% of AGI
    (4) Property taxes

    A. (1) and (2) only
    B. (1), (2), and (4) only
    C. (2), (3), and (4) only
    D. All of the above

78. All but which of the following are considered casualty losses?

    A. Sudden hail damage
    B. Termite infestation
    C. Damage to an automobile due to negligent driving
    D. All of the above are casualty losses.

79. All but which of the following are characteristics of an LLC?

    A. Limited liability to all members
    B. Dissolution upon the death, retirement, or resignation of a member unless the remaining members elect by majority to continue
    C. Majority approval required to transfer management or management rights
    D. Operating agreement is not required

80. All but which of the following are requirements for a valid prenuptial agreement?

    A. Both parties must provide full and complete disclosure of their net worth.
    B. The agreement must be in writing and signed by both parties.
    C. The agreement must be executed willingly by both parties without duress.
    D. The agreement must be intended to facilitate or promote the procurement of divorce.

81. Terry received gifted shares of ABC stock with an adjusted basis of $12,000. At the time of the gift, the fair market value of the stock was $7,000. Terry sold the stock for $10,000. What is the amount of capital gain or loss that Terry must recognize?

    A. $5,000 loss
    B. $2,000 loss
    C. $3,000 gain
    D. No gain or loss will be recognized.

82. Which of the following is/are correct regarding debt accumulated on a primary residence?

    (1) A taxpayer can deduct interest on a primary residence on a maximum indebtedness of $1 million.
    (2) A taxpayer can deduct interest on a maximum home equity loan of $100,000.

    A. (1) only
    B. (2) only
    C. None of the above
    D. All of the above

83. The maximum exclusion of gain on the sale of a principal residence is _____ for married couples filing jointly, and _____ for single taxpayers.

    A. $1,000,000, $500,000
    B. $500,000, $1,000,000
    C. $500,000, $250,000
    D. $250,000, $500,000

84. Child support payments are _____ to the payor and _____ to the recipient.

A. non-deductible, non-taxable
B. deductible, taxable
C. taxable, deductible
D. non-taxable, non-deductible

85. Which of the following is not a type of audit conducted by the IRS?

A. Field audit
B. Correspondence audit
C. Office audit
D. Court audit

86. Which of the following entities is subject to double taxation?

A. S Corp
B. C Corp
C. LLC
D. Partnership

For questions 87-96, choose the correct tax treatment for the items listed. Use only one answer per blank. Answers may be used more than once or not at all.

A. Included in income
B. Excluded from income

87. ____ Income earned on gifts

88. ____ Jury fees

89. ____ Royalties

90. ____ Forgiveness of debt through bankruptcy

91. ____ Income earned on inherited property

92. ____ Military combat pay

93. _____ Prizes

94. _____ Unemployment compensation

95. _____ Tips and gratuities

96. _____ Interest from municipal bonds used for public purposes

97. An improvement to a tangible asset has which of the following effects on the asset's basis?

    A. The cost of the improvement is added to the asset's basis.
    B. The cost of the improvement is subtracted from the asset's basis.
    C. The cost of the improvement does not change the asset's basis.
    D. None of the above are correct.

98. In a like-kind exchange, when property received by a related party is disposed of less than two years after the date of the exchange, what is the result?

    A. The like-kind exchange treatment is disallowed and the deferred gain is recognized over a two-year period.
    B. The like-kind exchange treatment is disallowed and the deferred gain is recognized for tax purposes immediately.
    C. The like-kind exchange treatment is permitted and the deferred gain is recognized for tax purposes immediately.
    D. The like-kind exchange treatment is permitted and the deferred gain does not need to be recognized.

99. How is a loss on the sale of a personal residence treated for tax purposes?

    A. Losses are unrecognized and non-deductible.
    B. Losses are unrecognized and non-deductible unless the ownership and use tests have been satisfied.
    C. Losses may be recognized up to $250,000 for single taxpayers and $500,000 for married taxpayers filing a joint tax return.
    D. Losses may be recognized as long-term capital losses.

100. Charitable donations are _____ to the extent the donor received consideration in return for the donation.

A. fully deductible
B. non-deductible
C. partially deductible
D. taxable

ANSWER KEY

1. B

In order to deduct alimony payments, the payments must be in cash and must end at the death of the payee. The payor and payee cannot live together.

2. A

For estimated tax payments, no penalty is imposed if the taxpayer did not have any income tax liability for the preceding year.

3. B

In order to deduct moving expenses, the distance between a taxpayer's new job and old residence must be at least 50 miles greater than the distance between the taxpayer's old job and old residence.

4. A

The more exemptions that are claimed on IRS Form W-4, the less tax is withheld from an employee's paycheck.

5. D

Secondary sources of tax information include periodicals, newsletters, books, and articles.

6. C

The penalty for failing to file a tax return is 5% of the tax due for each month the tax return is late, up to a maximum of 25%.

7. A

The penalty for negligence is 20% of the deficiency.

8. E

The penalty for filing a frivolous tax return is $500.

9. B

The penalty for civil fraud is 75% of the deficiency.

10. F

The penalty for aiding and abetting a tax liability understatement is $1,000.

11.A
The penalty for a substantial understatement of tax liability is 20% of the deficiency.

12. D
If a tax return has been filed but taxes have not been paid, the penalty is 0.5% of the tax due for each month the tax is unpaid, up to a maximum of 25%.

13. F
The penalty for promoting abusive tax shelters is $1,000 or 100% of gross income.

14. D
Above-the-line deductions include capital losses, deductible traditional IRA contributions, ordinary and necessary business (Schedule C) expenses, and alimony paid.

15. C
A refundable tax credit can reduce a taxpayer's income tax liability below zero. A non-refundable tax credit cannot reduce a taxpayer's income tax liability below zero.

16. B
The tests that must be met in order to claim a dependency tax exemption are the support test, member of household test, gross income test, joint return test, and citizenship test.

17. C
A CFP® without additional licensing is not permitted to represent a taxpayer when audited by the IRS.

18. D
There is a taxable wage base applied to the social security portion of a self-employed individual's income, above which amount the 12.4% tax does not need to be paid. There is no taxable wage base applied to the Medicare portion of a self-employed individual's income, and the 2.9% tax must always be paid.

19. C
Step 1: $50,000 x 0.0765 = $3,825
Step 2: $50,000 - $3,825 = $46,175
Step 3: $46,175 x 0.1530 = $7,065

20. D
According to the kiddie tax rules, if a child under the age of 19, or under the age of 24 if a full time student, has unearned income exceeding the annual threshold, the excess is taxed at the parent's marginal tax rate.

21. B
A taxpayer must receive approval from the IRS to change the accounting method or inventory reporting method used.

22. C
To be considered a long-term contract, the duties performed under the contract must not be completed within the same year in which construction begins.

23. D
When gifts of property are claimed as income tax deductions in excess of $5,000, the donor must obtain a qualified appraisal for each item donated and must include a copy of the appraisal with the tax return.

24. B
Non-business bad debts are deductible as short-term capital losses on Schedule D of IRS Form 1040. The amount deductible is limited to the taxpayer's basis in the debt.

25. D
A sole proprietorship provides unlimited liability for the owner.

26. B
The amount of Section 1244 stock that can be deducted as an ordinary loss is limited to $50,000 each year for a single taxpayer. On a joint tax return the limit is increased to $100,000.

27. A
IRS Form 1065 is an informational return used to report income, gains, losses, deductions, and credits from the operation of a partnership.

28. C
An S Corp may have up to 100 shareholders.

29. B
Any charitable contribution that is disallowed because of the limitation with respect to AGI can be carried forward for the lesser of 5 years or death, and may be deducted on the donor's future income tax returns.

30. C
A C Corp is potentially subject to the personal service corporation tax, accumulated earnings tax, and personal holding company tax.

31. A
If payments to an ex-spouse terminate when a child turns 18, rather than when the spouse remarries, the payments will be considered non-deductible and non-taxable child support.

32. B
The original basis of a newly acquired asset is equal to the cost plus expenses of sale, such as sales tax paid, installation costs, freight charges, and commissions incurred in acquiring the asset.

33. B
If an installment sale occurs and the buyer is a family member who then sells the purchased property within two years after acquiring it, the original seller must recognize all gain deferred by the installment sale in the year of the subsequent sale.

34. C
Depletion is the process by which the tax basis of natural resources is recovered.

35. A
Amortization is the process by which the tax basis of intangible assets is recovered.

36. B
Depreciation is the process by which the tax basis of tangible assets is recovered.

37. C
In a like-kind exchange, a taxpayer has 45 days after the date the relinquished property is transferred to identify potential replacement properties. The exchange must be completed within 180 days after the transfer of the relinquished property.

38. D
To satisfy the ownership test for the Section 121 exclusion, the home must have been owned and used as a principal residence for at least 2 of the 5 years preceding the date of sale.

39. C
A C Corp is subject to double taxation, has a perpetual life, and could potentially be classified as a personal service corporation (PSC).

40. D
Related parties include spouses, lineal descendants, brothers and sisters, a grantor and trustee of a trust, an executor and beneficiary of an estate, and an individual and corporation if the individual owns more than 50% of the value of outstanding stock.

41. B
AMT preference items and adjustments include the bargain element of incentive stock options (ISOs), private activity municipal bonds, oil and gas percentage depletion, and depreciation (ACRS and MACRS).

42. A
Government entities are public charities.

43. A
Churches and synagogues are public charities.

44. B
Fraternal organizations are private charities.

45. A
Educational organizations are public charities.

46. B
Veteran organizations are private charities.

47. A
Not-for-profit hospitals are public charities.

48. B
Private foundations are private charities.

49. D
The holding period of property inherited from a decedent is considered to always be long-term in nature. This is true even if the decedent had acquired the property only one day before his or her date of death.

50. B
Long-term capital gains tax rates apply if an asset is held for longer than 12 months (at least 12 months and a day).

51. D
A closely held C Corp will be classified as a PSC if it falls into one of the categories of the acronym "HEAL".
Health (doctors, dentists, etc.)
Engineering
Accounting, Architectural
Law

52. B
An itemized deduction is a personal expense that is permitted as a deduction from AGI in arriving at taxable income. It is a "below-the-line" deduction.

53. A
A C Corp would not provide flow-through taxation as the doctor requested. A sole proprietorship would not limit her liability. A limited partnership may be appropriate, but there is no mention of a general partner. The best answer is the S Corp.

54. B
The required annual tax payment is the lesser of 90% of the current year's estimated tax bill, or 100% of last year's tax bill. If last year's tax return reported income over $150,000, Jessica would have pay 110%, instead of 100%. The question states that Jessica expects her current year tax liability to be $25,000. She can pay 90% of $25,000, equal to $22,500.

55. A
The LLC and S Corp are pass-through entities which are not subject to graduated corporate tax rates. Any income retained by a personal service corporation (PSC) is taxed at a flat 35% rate. Only the C Corp is subject to graduated corporate tax rates.

56. C
In a limited partnership, the general partner has unlimited liability. The LLC, C Corp, and S Corp will protect investors from liability beyond the amount they personally invested.

57. C
Paying money to an ex-spouse's IRA pursuant to a divorce decree qualifies as alimony.

58. B
If Carl uses Mark's property as a rental property, then Carl can do a like-kind exchange. Carl is not disqualified from doing a like-kind exchange simply because Mark uses his property for non-business purposes. Mark cannot do a like-kind exchange because he currently owns a home, not a rental property.

59. B
Seth's overall charitable deduction is limited to 50% of AGI, or $75,000. Since the stock was held for less than one year, Seth's deduction is limited to the basis of $80,000. However, the 50% limit always applies, so only $75,000 can be deducted this year. The excess $5,000 is carried forward to next year.

60. D
A deduction is more beneficial to a high-bracket taxpayer, and a credit is more beneficial to a low-bracket taxpayer.

61. D
A home can be rented up to 14 days per year without any tax consequences.

62. D
Stephanie will have to pay individual income tax plus self-employment tax (social security and Medicare tax) on her independent contractor income.

63. C
The owner is permitted to deduct losses up to his basis of $85,000 ($55,000 + $30,000).

64. A
To determine the loss on the sale of a gift, the donee's basis is the lower of the donor's basis or the fair market value of the property when the donee receives it. Although Tim's basis was $9,000, the value of the gift when John received it was only $5,000, which becomes his new basis. Therefore, John realized a $2,000 loss when he sold the painting for $3,000.

65. C
In order to use the home office deduction, the office must be either the taxpayer's principal place of business, or where he or she meets with patients or clients in the normal course of business.

66. B
Alimony is taxable to the payee and deductible by the payor. Premiums paid on up to $50,000 of group term life insurance are not considered taxable income to an employee. However, the question states that coverage is for $75,000. Therefore, a portion will be taxable. Child support payments and workers compensation are not taxable income.

67. B
This is a bargain sale to charity. The taxable gain is calculated as follows:
Step 1: $300,000 (sale price) / $900,000 (FMV) = 33%
Step 2: 33% x $100,000 (basis) = $33,333
Step 3: $300,000 (sale price) - $33,333 = $266,667 taxable gain

68. C
Gambling losses to the extent of winnings are not subject to the 2% of AGI floor.

69. A
When property is transferred for less than full consideration of money or money's worth, the value of the gift is equal to the value of the property transferred less the consideration received.

70. A
The majority of individual tax returns filed in the US use the cash method of accounting.

71. C
The tax rate structure being used to tax Mike and Mary is progressive.

72. B
A taxpayer may petition for redetermination of an assessed income tax penalty and receive a jury trial in US District Court.

73. C
Kate's tax filing status for the current year is married filing jointly.

74. B
Capital losses have a three-year carry back period, and a five-year carry forward period.

75. B
The maximum amount of capital loss that a single taxpayer can deduct in a single year is up to the amount of capital gain plus $3,000.

76. A
A wash sale occurs when an investor acquires substantially identical stock during the 30 days prior to, or 30 days after the date of sale.

77. A
In calculating alternative minimum taxable income (AMTI), a taxpayer can deduct casualty losses in excess of 10% of AGI, and qualified personal residence interest. Only medical expenses in excess of 10% of AGI can be deducted.

78. B
A casualty loss can only result from the damage, destruction, or loss of property from a sudden event. A termite infestation is not considered a sudden event.

79. D
An operating agreement is required to determine the management structure of an LLC.

80. D
A prenuptial agreement must not be intended to facilitate or promote the procurement of divorce.

81. D
No gain or loss will be recognized when Terry sells the stock.

82. D
A taxpayer can deduct interest on a primary residence on a maximum indebtedness of $1 million, and can deduct interest on a maximum home equity loan of $100,000.

83. C
The maximum exclusion of gain on the sale of a principal residence is $500,000 for married couples filing jointly, and $250,000 for single taxpayers.

84. A
Child support payments are non-deductible to the payor and non-taxable to the recipient.

85. D
Three types of audits conducted by the IRS are field audits, correspondence audits, and office audits.

86. B
A C Corp is subject to double taxation. Earnings are taxed once at the entity level and again at the individual level once distributions have occurred.

87. A
Income earned on gifts is included in income.

88. A
Jury fees are included in income.

89. A
Royalties are included in income.

90. B
Forgiveness of debt through bankruptcy is excluded from income. However, forgiveness of debt, other than through bankruptcy, is included in income.

91. A
Income earned on inherited property is included in income.

92. B
Military combat pay is excluded from income.

93. A
Prizes are included in income.

94. A
Unemployment compensation is included in income.

95. A
Tips and gratuities are included in income.

96. B

Interest from municipal bonds used for public purposes is excluded from income.

97. A

The cost of an improvement to a tangible asset is added to the asset's basis.

98. B

In a like-kind exchange, when property received by a related party is disposed of less than two years after the date of the exchange, the like-kind exchange treatment is disallowed and the deferred gain is recognized for tax purposes immediately.

99. A

A loss on the sale of a personal residence is unrecognized and non-deductible, even if the ownership and use tests have been satisfied by the taxpayer.

100. B

Donations are non-deductible to the extent the donor received consideration in return for the donation.

INVESTMENTS

QUESTIONS

1. Which of the following is correct regarding certificates of deposit (CDs)?

   A. CDs are short-term securities that may be bought or sold in the open market at a market-determined price.

   B. CDs typically invest in high-quality, short-term investments, such as commercial paper, T-Bills, and money market funds.

   C. CDs are known as "time deposits".

   D. The financial institution pays a variable rate of interest for the term of the CD.

2. All but which of the following are correct regarding Treasury bills?

   A. Have maturities of one year or less

   B. Sold in minimum denominations of $500

   C. Considered to be default risk free

   D. Sold at a discount to par

3. Which of the following describes the relationship between total risk, systematic risk, and unsystematic risk?

   A. Total risk = systematic risk − unsystematic risk

   B. Total risk − systematic risk = unsystematic risk

   C. Unsystematic risk − total risk = systematic risk

   D. Total risk + unsystematic risk = systematic risk

4. Common stock is referred to as _____ because the owner of the stock is also an owner of the corporation and may participate in its capital and income growth.

   A. debt

   B. equity

   C. cumulative stock

   D. preferred stock

5. Which of the following are correct regarding a bond's yield to maturity (YTM)?

(1) The YTM assumes that coupon payments are reinvested at the YTM rate of return for the life of the bond.
(2) When the market rate of interest for the same term and risk is higher than the coupon rate, a discount will be priced into the bond.
(3) Bonds that are riskier will have lower yields to maturity.
(4) The YTM is the internal rate of return for cash flow associated with a bond, including the purchase price, coupon payments, and maturity value.

A. (1) and (2) only
B. (3) and (4) only
C. (1), (2), and (4) only
D. (1), (3), and (4) only

6. An investment grade bond is one that is rated _____ or higher by the Standard & Poor's bond rating service. A high-yield bond is rated _____ or lower by Standard & Poor's.

A. BBB, BB
B. BBB+, BB-
C. BBB-, BB+
D. BB, BBB

7. Which of the following describes bonds that have a legal claim to specific assets in the event of default, insolvency, or liquidation?

A. Debenture bonds
B. Secured bonds
C. Unsecured bonds
D. Indenture bonds

8. Which of the following are characteristics of EE bonds?

(1) May be purchased for an amount that is equal to one-half of face value
(2) May be purchased for a minimum price of $25 for a $50 bond
(3) US Treasury guarantees an EE bond's value will double after 10 years
(4) May be purchased for a maximum price of $5,000 for a $10,000 bond

A. (1) only
B. (1), (2), and (4) only
C. (2), (3), and (4) only
D. All of the above

9. Which of the following are characteristics of zero-coupon bonds?

(1) A zero-coupon bond does not make periodic interest payments throughout the term of the bond.
(2) Zero-coupon bonds have significant reinvestment risk because no payments are made until the bond matures.
(3) Zero-coupon bonds require taxes to be paid currently on accrued interest each year, even though no interest is received.
(4) The duration of a zero-coupon bond is less than its term to maturity.

A. (1) and (3) only
B. (2) and (4) only
C. (1), (2), and (3) only
D. (2), (3), and (4) only

For questions 10-19, match the type of stock with the description that follows. Use only one answer per blank. Answers may be used more than once or not at all.

A. Cyclical stocks
B. Interest sensitive stocks
C. Defensive stocks

10. _____ Pharmaceutical companies

11. _____ Automobiles

12. _____ Insurance companies

13. ____ Airlines

14. ____ Railroads

15. ____ Utilities

16. ____ Tobacco companies

17. ____ Steel companies

18. ____ Savings and loans

19. ____ Commercial banks

20. All but which of the following are characteristics of exchange-traded funds (ETFs)?

   A. Traded on an exchange like individual securities
   B. Trades settle at the end of the trading day, similar to mutual funds
   C. Lower expenses than mutual funds
   D. Income tax efficient

21. If a corporation is required to pay unpaid dividends from prior years before paying a dividend to common stockholders, the stock is considered to be which of the following?

   A. Accumulated preferred stock
   B. Preferred stock
   C. Convertible stock
   D. Cumulative preferred stock

22. **Which of the following is/are correct regarding the capital structure of open-end mutual funds?**

(1) Open-end mutual funds issue new shares and redeem existing shares from share-holders.
(2) The price an investor pays when buying shares of an open-end mutual fund is based on supply and demand.

A. (1) only
B. (2) only
C. None of the above
D. All of the above

23. **How is the net asset value (NAV) of a mutual fund calculated?**

A. NAV = (total value of investment + liabilities) / shares outstanding
B. NAV = (total value of investment / shares outstanding) - liabilities
C. NAV = (total value of investment − liabilities) / shares outstanding
D. NAV = total value of investment / shares outstanding

24. **A hedge fund is a _____ offered fund of securities for wealthy investors. The investment manager is generally paid a _____ fee.**

A. publicly, performance
B. privately, performance
C. publicly, flat
D. privately, flat

25. **Which of the following are characteristics of guaranteed investment contracts (GICs)?**

(1) GICs are sold by insurance companies primarily to mutual fund companies.
(2) GICs provide higher returns than savings accounts and US Treasury securities.
(3) The rate of return is guaranteed for a fixed period of time, such as five years.
(4) Returns for GICs are generally lower than equities because little risk is involved.

A. (1) and (3) only
B. (2) and (4) only
C. (2), (3), and (4) only
D. All of the above

26. All but which of the following are characteristics of a REIT?

A. A REIT is a publicly traded open-end investment company.
B. A mortgage REIT is a specific type of REIT.
C. A REIT can sell at a premium or discount to its NAV.
D. All of the above are correct.

27. Which of the following is/are correct regarding cyclical stocks?

(1) When the economy is growing, demand usually strengthens and cyclical companies are able to make large profits.
(2) When the economy is declining, cyclical companies are hurt by decreases in demand and are less profitable.

A. (1) only
B. (2) only
C. None of the above
D. All of the above

28. Puts are an option to _____ a specified number of shares of stock during a specified period at a specified price. A buyer of a put option expects the price of the underlying stock to _____.

A. buy, fall
B. sell, rise
C. buy, rise
D. sell, fall

29. Which of the following accurately describes the difference between rights and warrants?

(1) A warrant may be attached to new debt or preferred issues to make the issues more attractive to buyers.
(2) A difference between rights and warrants is their lifespan.
(3) Warrants usually expire within a few weeks.
(4) Rights may continue without expiring for up to several years.

A. (1) only
B. (1) and (2) only
C. (2), (3), and (4) only
D. All of the above

30. Which of the following is not a characteristic of tangible assets, such as collectibles?

A. Collectibles do not have a strong secondary market.
B. Collectibles are not subject to significant government regulation.
C. Collectibles are marketable.
D. Collectibles lack liquidity.

For questions 31-40, match the type of risk with the description that follows. Use only one answer per blank. Answers may be used more than once or not at all.

A. Systematic risk
B. Unsystematic risk

31. _____ Purchasing power risk

32. _____ Business risk

33. _____ Market risk

34. _____ Financial risk

35. _____ Interest rate risk

36. _____ Exchange rate risk

37. _____ Default risk

38. _____ Political risk

39. _____ Reinvestment risk

40. _____ Tax risk

41. Which of the following measures how far the actual outcomes of a probability distribution deviate from the arithmetic mean?

A. Skewness
B. Correlation coefficient
C. Coefficient of determination
D. Poisson distribution

42. The Jensen and Treynor ratios assume a _____ portfolio. The Sharpe ratio assumes a _____ portfolio.

A. non-diversified, diversified
B. non-diversified, riskless
C. diversified, non-diversified
D. riskless, diversified

43. Which of the following is/are correct regarding beta?

(1) Beta is used to measure the amount of unsystematic risk in an investor's portfolio.
(2) A portfolio's beta can be positive or equal to zero, but cannot be negative.

A. (1) only
B. (2) only
C. None of the above
D. All of the above

44. When a bond is selling at a premium to par, the YTM will always be _____ the bond's coupon rate. If a bond is selling at a discount to par, the YTM will always be _____ the bond's coupon rate.

A. greater than, less than
B. less than, greater than
C. greater than, equal to
D. less than, equal to

45. Which of the following describes a strategy used to minimize the interest rate risk of bond investments by adjusting the portfolio duration to match the investment time horizon?

A. Bond laddering
B. Bond immunization
C. Bond hedging
D. Bond spread

For questions 46-48, select the relationship that best describes the bond characteristics provided. Use only one answer per blank. Answers may be used more than once or not at all.

A. Inverse relationship
B. Direct relationship

46. _____ The coupon rate of a bond and its duration

47. _____ The maturity date of a bond and its duration

48. _____ The YTM of a bond and its duration

49. Assume that ABC stock pays a constant dividend of $5 per share each year. The dividend is not expected to grow. Also assume that an investor has a required rate of return of 10%. What is the intrinsic value of ABC stock?

A. $10 per share
B. $25 per share
C. $50 per share
D. $60 per share

50. According to Modern Portfolio Theory, an investor's optimal portfolio is located at the point of tangency of the investor's _____ and the _____ of available investment assets.

   A. marginal utility curve, efficient frontier
   B. optimal portfolio, efficient frontier
   C. indifference curve, efficient frontier
   D. marginal utility curve, indifference curve

51. According to the anomaly known as the small-firm effect, _____ companies have been shown to outperform _____ companies on a risk-adjusted basis over a period of many years.

   A. large cap, small cap
   B. mid cap, small cap
   C. small cap, large cap
   D. small cap, mid cap

For questions 52-54, select the word that best completes the bond relationship provided. Use only one answer per blank. Answers may be used more than once or not at all.

   A. More
   B. Less

52. ____ Lower-coupon bonds are _____ affected by interest rate changes than higher-coupon bonds.

53. ____ Long-term bonds are _____ affected by interest rate changes than short-term bonds.

54. ____ The shorter a bond's term to maturity, the _____ its potential for relative price fluctuation.

55. According to the principles of behavioral finance, which theory suggests that investors typically fear losses more than they value gains? As a result, investors will often choose the smaller of two potential gains if it avoids a highly probable loss.

    A. Expected utility theory
    B. Prospect theory
    C. Game theory
    D. Zero sum theory

56. A large interest rate change has the most significant effect on a _____ bond.

    A. low coupon
    B. short duration
    C. high coupon
    D. short maturity

For questions 57-66, match the ratio with the description that follows. Use only one answer per blank. Answers may be used more than once or not at all.

    A. Inventory turnover ratio
    B. Current ratio
    C. Net profit margin
    D. Quick ratio
    E. Operating profit margin
    F. Return on equity
    G. Fixed asset turnover ratio
    H. Debt-to-equity ratio
    I. Average collection period
    J. Return on assets

57. _____ Current assets divided by current liabilities

58. _____ Annual sales divided by average inventory level

59. _____ Earnings before interest and taxes (EBIT) divided by annual sales

60. _____ Current assets less inventory divided by current liabilities

61. _____ Earnings after taxes divided by total assets

62. ____ Annual receivables divided by sales per day

63. ____ Annual sales divided by fixed assets

64. ____ Total debt divided by common stockholder equity

65. ____ Earnings after taxes divided by annual sales

66. ____ Earnings after taxes divided by common stockholder equity

67. All but which of the following are charting techniques used by technical analysts?

A. Moving average
B. Trendline
C. CAPM
D. Support and resistance levels

68. The initial margin percentage is currently _____ as established by Regulation T of the Federal Reserve Board.

A. 25%
B. 30%
C. 50%
D. 75%

69. Which of the following factors are included in the Arbitrage Pricing Theory (APT)?

(1) Unexpected inflation
(2) Unexpected changes in industrial production
(3) Unexpected shifts in risk premiums
(4) Unexpected changes in interest rates

A. (1) and (2) only
B. (1), (3), and (4) only
C. (2), (3), and (4) only
D. All of the above

For questions 70-72, match the dividend date with the description that follows. Use only one answer per blank. Answers may be used more than once or not at all.

A. Date of declaration
B. Ex-dividend date
C. Date of record
D. Date of payment

70. _____ The date it is determined who owns stock in the company and is entitled to receive a dividend.

71. _____ The date the board of directors approves and decides that a dividend will be paid.

72. _____ The date the market price of the stock adjusts for the dividend.

73. The standard deviation of an investor's portfolio must be _____ the weighted average of the standard deviation of returns of the individual securities.

A. equal to
B. less than or equal to
C. less than
D. greater than

74. All but which of the following are underlying assumptions of the capital asset pricing model (CAPM)?

A. All investors have the same one-period time horizon.
B. All investors have the same expectations about the risk-return relationship of assets.
C. Investors can borrow and lend at a specific risk-free rate of return equal to zero.
D. There are no transaction costs, taxes, or inflation.

75. Which of the following is/are correct regarding a bond's coupon rate?

   (1) The smaller a bond's coupon, the greater its relative price fluctuation.
   (2) The smaller a bond's coupon, the greater its reinvestment risk.

   A. (1) only
   B. (2) only
   C. None of the above
   D. All of the above

76. Buying a _____ and selling a _____ are both bullish strategies.

   A. put, call
   B. put, put
   C. call, call
   D. call, put

77. In analyzing a mutual fund, if the standard deviation is high, R^2 is 0.25, alpha is high, and beta is 0.85, which of the following is correct?

   A. Alpha is significant
   B. Beta is significant
   C. The Sharpe calculation is significant
   D. The Treynor calculation is significant

78. Which of the following describes the rate of return calculated by the capital asset pricing model (CAPM)?

   A. The rate of return is not reliable because CAPM fails to take risk into account.
   B. The rate of return can be used in the dividend growth model for valuing common stock.
   C. The rate of return represents the stock market's overall rate of return.
   D. The rate of return is not reliable because CAPM uses beta in its formula.

79. Which of the following are liquidity ratios?

(1) Current ratio
(2) Debt-to-equity ratio
(3) Quick ratio
(4) Fixed asset turnover ratio

A. (1) and (2) only
B. (1) and (3) only
C. (2), (3), and (4) only
D. All of the above

80. Based on the Markowitz model, which of the following securities would a rational investor select?

A. Rate of return 4%, beta 1.3
B. Rate of return 7%, beta 1.1
C. Rate of return 6%, beta 1.2
D. Rate of return 7%, beta 1.2

81. The duration of a bond is least affected by which of the following characteristics?

A. Coupon
B. Time to maturity
C. Interest rate
D. Quality

82. Which of the following will shift the Markowitz efficient frontier upward and to the left?

A. Selecting investments with lower coefficients of correlation between them
B. Changing the proportion of securities already invested in the portfolio
C. Taking less risk
D. Taking more risk

83. If an investor expects a large decrease in the stock market sixty days from today, she can take advantage of the change by doing which of the following?

(1) Buying S&P 500 index calls
(2) Buying S&P 500 index puts
(3) Selling S&P 500 index calls
(4) Selling S&P 500 index puts

A. (1) and (3) only
B. (1) and (4) only
C. (2) and (3) only
D. (2) and (4) only

84. A mutual fund that invests in securities both inside and outside the US is known as a/ an _____ .

A. long-short fund
B. balanced fund
C. international fund
D. global fund

85. Which of the following securities are backed by the full faith and credit of the US government?

A. Student Loan Marketing Association notes (Sallie Maes)
B. Federal Home Loan Mortgage Corporation debentures (Freddie Macs)
C. Federal National Mortgage Association certificates (Fannie Maes)
D. Government National Mortgage Association certificates (Ginnie Maes)

86. **Which of the following investments will provide tax-exempt interest if the proceeds are used to pay for qualifying education expenses?**

    (1) FNMA funds
    (2) EE bonds
    (3) Treasury bonds
    (4) Treasury bills

    A. (2) only
    B. (1) and (2) only
    C. (2), (3), and (4) only
    D. All of the above

87. **Which of the following is correct regarding non-systematic risk?**

    A. It includes such risks as tax risk and financial risk.
    B. An investor who owns five growth common stocks can reduce non-systematic risk by adding value common stocks to her portfolio.
    C. It is the risk associated with a particular security or company.
    D. All of the above are correct.

88. **When an investment company puts home mortgages or other loans into a pool and then sells securities representing shares of the pool, the securities sold are referred to as which of the following?**

    A. Donor advised funds
    B. Pooled income funds
    C. Derivative-backed securities
    D. Asset-backed securities

89. Eurodollars have which of the following characteristics?

(1) Eurodollars are foreign denominated deposits in banks located outside the US.
(2) Eurodollars involve deposits made at only European banks.

A. (1) only
B. (2) only
C. None of the above
D. All of the above

90. Which of the following is/are correct regarding registered bonds and bearer bonds?

(1) A registered bond is registered with the corporation or organization that issued the bond, and coupon payments are made to the owner of record.
(2) A bearer bond can be transferred like cash, and coupon payments are made to the person who holds the bond.

A. (1) only
B. (2) only
C. None of the above
D. All of the above

91. Which of the following is/are correct regarding interest paid from municipal bonds?

(1) Interest paid from municipal bonds is not taxed by the federal government.
(2) Interest paid from municipal bonds is never taxable at the state level.

A. (1) only
B. (2) only
C. None of the above
D. All of the above

92. Which of the following is an unconditional promise to pay a sum of money to a payee, either at a fixed or determinable future time, under specific terms?

A. IOU
B. Promissory note
C. Bank draft
D. None of the above are correct.

For questions 93-96, match the stock hedging technique with the description that follows. Use only one answer per blank. Answers may be used more than once or not at all.

A. Collar
B. Spread
C. Straddle
D. Protective put

93. _____ Purchasing a call option and selling a call option on the same stock at the same time

94. _____ Purchasing a put option and selling a call option on the same stock at the same time

95. _____ Purchasing a put option while holding shares of the underlying stock from a previous purchase

96. _____ Purchasing a call option and a put option on the same stock at the same time

97. The purpose of the Black-Scholes valuation model is to determine the value of a _____ option of a _____ paying stock.

A. call, dividend
B. call, non-dividend
C. put, dividend
D. put, non-dividend

98. The duration of a coupon bond is always _____ its term to maturity. A zero-coupon bond's duration is always _____ its term to maturity.

A. less than, greater than
B. greater than, less than
C. less than, equal to
D. equal to, less than

99. In a short call, the maximum gain is _____ and the maximum loss is _____.

A. unlimited, the premium
B. the premium, unlimited
C. unlimited, unlimited
D. limited, limited

100. Which of the following investment strategies is profitable in a declining stock market?

(1) Buying a call
(2) Buying a put
(3) Selling a put
(4) Selling a call

A. (1) and (3) only
B. (1) and (4) only
C. (2) and (3) only
D. (2) and (4) only

ANSWER KEY

1. C

Certificates of deposit (CDs) are known as "time deposits". They are deposits made with a bank for a specified period of time.

2. B

Treasury bills are sold in minimum denominations of $1,000.

3. B

Total risk = systematic risk + unsystematic risk.
This formula can be rewritten as: Total risk − systematic risk = unsystematic risk.

4. B

Common stock is referred to as equity because the owner of the stock is also an owner of the corporation and may participate in its capital and income growth.

5. C

Bonds that are riskier will have higher yields to maturity.

6. C

An investment grade bond is one that is rated BBB- or higher by the Standard & Poor's bond rating service. A high-yield bond is rated BB+ or lower by Standard & Poor's.

7. B

Secured bonds have a legal claim to specific assets in the event of default, insolvency, or liquidation.

8. B

At a minimum, the US Treasury guarantees an EE bond's value will double after 20 years.

9. A

A zero-coupon bond has no reinvestment risk. The duration of a zero-coupon bond is equal to its term to maturity.

10. C

Pharmaceutical companies are defensive stocks.

11. A
Automobiles are cyclical stocks.

12. B
Insurance companies are interest sensitive stocks.

13. A
Airlines are cyclical stocks.

14. A
Railroads are cyclical stocks.

15. B
Utilities are interest sensitive stocks.

16. C
Tobacco companies are defensive stocks.

17. A
Steel companies are cyclical stocks.

18. B
Savings and loans are interest sensitive stocks.

19. B
Commercial banks are interest sensitive stocks.

20. B
ETFs may be bought or sold throughout the trading day like individual securities.

21. D
If a corporation is required to pay unpaid dividends from prior years before paying a dividend to common stockholders, the stock is referred to as cumulative preferred stock.

22. A
The price an investor pays when buying shares of an open-end mutual fund is based on the fund's net asset value (NAV).

23. C
NAV = (total value of investment – liabilities) / shares outstanding

24. B

A hedge fund is a privately offered fund of securities for wealthy investors. The investment manager is generally paid a performance fee.

25. C

Guaranteed investment contracts (GICs) are sold by insurance companies primarily to pension plans.

26. A

REITs are publicly traded closed-end investment companies.

27. D

Cyclical stocks tend to prosper in growing and expanding economies, and do poorly during down business cycles.

28. D

Puts are an option to sell a specified number of shares of stock during a specified period at a specified price. A buyer of a put option expects the price of the underlying stock to fall.

29. B

Rights usually expire within a few weeks. Warrants may continue without expiring for up to several years.

30. C

Collectibles lack marketability and liquidity.

31. A

Purchasing power risk is a type of systematic risk.

32. B

Business risk is a type of unsystematic risk.

33. A

Market risk is a type of systematic risk.

34. B

Financial risk is a type of unsystematic risk.

35. A

Interest rate risk is a type of systematic risk.

36. A
Exchange rate risk is a type of systematic risk.

37. B
Default risk is a type of unsystematic risk.

38. B
Political risk is a type of unsystematic risk.

39. A
Reinvestment risk is a type of systematic risk.

40. B
Tax risk is a type of unsystematic risk.

41. A
Skewness measures how far the actual outcomes of a probability distribution deviate from the arithmetic mean.

42. C
The Jensen and Treynor ratios assume a diversified portfolio. The Sharpe ratio assumes a non-diversified portfolio.

43. C
Beta is used to measure the amount of systematic risk in an investor's portfolio. A portfolio's beta can be positive, negative, or equal to zero.

44. B
When a bond is selling at a premium to par, the YTM will always be less than the bond's coupon rate. If a bond is selling at a discount to par, the YTM will always be greater than the bond's coupon rate.

45. B
Bond immunization is an investment strategy used to minimize the interest rate risk of bond investments by adjusting the portfolio duration to match the investment time horizon.

46. A
There is an inverse relationship between the coupon rate of a bond and its duration. Therefore, the lower the coupon rate, the greater the bond's duration.

47. B
There is a direct relationship between the maturity date of a bond and its duration. Therefore, the longer the term to maturity, the greater the bond's duration.

48. A
There is an inverse relationship between the YTM of a bond and its duration. Therefore, the lower the YTM, the greater the bond's duration.

49. C
Intrinsic value of ABC stock = ($5 / 0.10) = $50 per share

50. C
According to Modern Portfolio Theory, a client's optimal portfolio is located at the point of tangency of the investor's indifference curve and the efficient frontier of available investment assets.

51. C
According to the anomaly known as the small-firm effect, small cap companies have been shown to outperform large cap companies on a risk-adjusted basis over a period of many years.

52. A
Lower-coupon bonds are more affected by interest rate changes than higher-coupon bonds. Lower-coupon bonds have more price volatility.

53. A
Long-term bonds are more affected by interest rate changes than short-term bonds. Long-term bonds have more price volatility.

54. B
The shorter a bond's term to maturity, the less its potential for relative price fluctuation. Long-term bonds have more price volatility.

55. B
Prospect theory suggests that investors typically fear losses more than they value gains. As a result, investors will often choose the smaller of two potential gains if it avoids a highly probable loss.

56. A
A large interest rate change has the most significant effect on a low coupon bond.

57. B
Current ratio = current assets divided by current liabilities

58. A
Inventory turnover ratio = annual sales divided by average inventory level

59. E
Operating profit margin = earnings before interest and taxes (EBIT) divided by annual sales

60. D
Quick ratio = current assets less inventory divided by current liabilities

61. J
Return on assets = earnings after taxes divided by total assets

62. I
Average collection period = annual receivables divided by sales per day

63. G
Fixed asset turnover ratio = annual sales divided by fixed assets

64. H
Debt-to-equity ratio = total debt divided by common stockholder equity

65. C
Net profit margin = earnings after taxes divided by annual sales

66. F
Return on equity = earnings after taxes divided by common stockholder equity

67. C
Technical analysts use charting techniques which include the moving average, trendline, and support and resistance levels.

68. C
The initial margin percentage is currently 50% as established by Regulation T of the Federal Reserve Board.

69. D
The factors included in the Arbitrage Pricing Theory (APT) are unexpected inflation, unexpected changes in industrial production, unexpected shifts in risk premiums, and unexpected changes in interest rates.

70. C

The date of record is the date a company determines who owns stock in the company and is entitled to receive a dividend.

71. A

The date of declaration is the date the board of directors approves and decides that a dividend will be paid.

72. B

The ex-dividend date is the date the market price of the stock adjusts for the dividend.

73. B

The standard deviation of an investor's portfolio must be less than or equal to the weighted average of the standard deviation of returns of the individual securities.

74. C

In the capital asset pricing model (CAPM) the risk-free rate of return may be greater than zero.

75. A

The smaller a bond's coupon, the greater its relative price fluctuation. The smaller a bond's coupon, the lower its reinvestment risk.

76. D

Buying a call and selling a put are both bullish strategies.

77. C

R^2 is the coefficient of determination and a measure of systematic risk. If R^2 is high (>0.60), then beta is the relevant measure to use when comparing securities. The beta measures are alpha and Treynor. If R^2 is low (<0.60), then standard deviation is the relevant measure to use when comparing securities. The standard deviation measure is Sharpe.

78. B

CAPM calculates the required rate of return for a stock based on its beta and the stock market's overall rate of return. That rate of return can then be used in the dividend growth model to value common stock.

79. B

The liquidity ratios are the current ratio and quick ratio.

80. B

B is the answer by process of elimination. Begin with the securities with a beta of 1.2 and select the one with the highest return. This eliminates security C. Next, compare the securities that have an investment return of 7% and select the one with the least risk (lowest beta). This eliminates security D. Finally, compare the two securities that remain, A and B. Security B provides a higher return for less risk than security A. Therefore, security B is the investment a rational investor would select.

81. D

A bond's quality does not directly impact its duration.

82. A

Taking more or less risk will move an investor's position along the efficient frontier, but will not shift it. The same is true of changing the proportion of securities already invested in a portfolio. However, by selecting investments with lower coefficients of correlation, the risk will be reduced and the efficient frontier will shift upward and to the left.

83. C

If an investor expects a large decrease in the stock market sixty days from today, she can take advantage of the change by buying S&P 500 index puts and selling S&P 500 index calls.

84. D

A mutual fund that invests in securities both inside and outside the US is known as a global fund.

85. D

Only Government National Mortgage Association certificates (Ginnie Maes) are backed by the full faith and credit of the US government.

86. A

EE Bonds provide tax-exempt interest if the proceeds are used to pay for qualifying education expenses.

87. D

All of the items listed describe non-systematic risk.

88. D

When an investment company puts home mortgages or other loans into a pool and then sells securities representing shares of the pool, the securities sold are referred to as asset-backed securities.

89. C

Eurodollars are US dollar denominated deposits in banks located outside the US. They do not involve deposits at only European banks.

90. D

A registered bond is registered with the corporation or organization that issued the bond, and coupon payments are made to the owner of record. A bearer bond can be transferred like cash, and coupon payments are made to the person who holds the bond.

91. A

Interest paid from municipal bonds is not taxed by the federal government. The bond interest may also be tax-exempt by various states if certain requirements are met.

92. B

A promissory note is an unconditional promise to pay a sum of money to a payee, either at a fixed or determinable future time, under specific terms. An IOU differs from a promissory note in that an IOU does not specify repayment terms such as the time of repayment. A bank draft is a type of check in which the payment is guaranteed to be available by the issuing bank.

93. B

A spread is the simultaneous purchase of one option and the sale of another option on the same side or position within the market. For example, purchasing a call option and selling a call option on the same stock at the same time is a spread

94. A

A collar is a technique used to protect an investor's gain in a long position of stock. Specifically, an investor purchases a put option to protect against a decline in the value of an underlying stock, and sells a call option to generate premium income to cover the cost of the put option premium.

95. D

In a protective put, an investor purchases a put option while holding shares of an underlying stock from a previous purchase.

96. C

A straddle is the simultaneous purchase of a call option and a put option on the same stock at the same time.

97. B

The purpose of the Black-Scholes valuation model is to determine the value of a call option of a non-dividend paying stock.

98. C

The duration of a coupon bond is always less than its term to maturity. A zero-coupon bond's duration is always equal to its term to maturity.

99. B

In a short call, the maximum gain is the premium and the maximum loss is unlimited.

100. D

Buying a put and selling a call are bearish strategies. Investors choose these options when they expect the stock market to decline in value.

RETIREMENT AND EMPLOYEE BENEFITS

QUESTIONS

1. Early withdrawals from a **SIMPLE IRA** are subject to a _____ penalty if the withdrawals are made during the first two years of plan participation.

    A. 10%
    B. 15%
    C. 20%
    D. 25%

2. All but which of the following groups are covered under social security?

    (1) Clergy
    (2) Federal employees hired before 1984
    (3) Railroad employees
    (4) Newspaper delivery persons under age 18

    A. (1) and (3) only
    B. (1), (2), and (4) only
    C. (2), (3), and (4) only
    D. All of the above

3. The two broad categories of defined contribution plans are:

    A. qualified plans and nonqualified plans.
    B. profit sharing plans and pension plans.
    C. personal plans and employer plans.
    D. defined benefit plans and pension plans.

4. Hardship withdrawals taken from a 401k plan before age 59 ½ typically require _____ of plan participation.

    A. 6 months
    B. 9 months
    C. 1 year
    D. 2 years

5. Which of the following are characteristics of stock bonus plans?

(1) Protects company stock from hostile takeovers
(2) Provides a market for the owner's closely held shares of stock
(3) Provides a tax advantage to employees through net unrealized appreciation
(4) Provides tax deductions while having no effect on cash flow

A. (1) and (2) only
B. (1), (3), and (4) only
C. (2), (3), and (4) only
D. All of the above

6. Which of the following is/are correct regarding loans from a 401k plan?

(1) A loan from a 401k plan cannot exceed $50,000 or 50% of the participant's vested benefit.
(2) If a participant's vested amount is $15,000 or less, the entire amount can be made available for loan without regard to the 50% restriction.

A. (1) only
B. (2) only
C. None of the above
D. All of the above

7. The cost of employer-provided life insurance coverage up to _____ on dependents is excludible from income as a de minimis fringe benefit. The cost of coverage over the threshold is fully taxable to the employee.

A. $1,000
B. $2,000
C. $10,000
D. $50,000

8. Hardship withdrawals taken from a 401k plan are subject to a _____ premature distribution penalty.

A. 0%
B. 5%
C. 10%
D. 15%

9. Which of the following is granted to an employee at no cost or at a bargain price with restrictions, such as the stock cannot be sold or disposed of before a specified period of time?

A. Junior stock
B. Restricted stock
C. Phantom stock
D. Stock appreciation rights

10. Defined benefit plans tend to favor older employees for which of the following reasons?

A. The future value of the participant's promised benefit is greater the less time remaining until retirement.
B. The present value of the participant's promised benefit is greater the less time remaining until retirement.
C. The future value of the participant's promised benefit is greater the more time remaining until retirement.
D. The present value of the participant's promised benefit is greater the more time remaining until retirement.

For questions 11-13, determine how the annual cost of a defined benefit plan will be effected by the scenario provided. Use only one answer per blank. Answers may be used more than once or not at all.

A. Higher annual cost
B. Lower annual cost
C. No effect

11. _____ **Higher than expected turnover**

12. _____ **Longer life expectancy**

13. _____ **Higher than expected investment returns**

14. **The rules for a qualified domestic relations order (QDRO) apply to all but which of the following plans?**

A. 401k plan
B. Nonqualified plan
C. 403b plan
D. 457 plan

15. **A benefit plan is considered to be _____ if an employee has only the employer's promise to pay an amount sometime in the future out of future cash flow.**

A. funded
B. informally funded
C. conditionally funded
D. unfunded

16. **Which of the following government agencies are responsible for monitoring qualified retirement plan rules and eligibility?**

A. ERISA and the IRS
B. IRS and the Department of Labor
C. IRS and the PBGC
D. ERISA and the PBGC

17. Employees must be eligible to participate in a 401k plan within _____ after the later of attaining age 21 or completing 1 year of service.

   A. 3 months
   B. 6 months
   C. 9 months
   D. 1 year

18. For the substantially equal periodic payment (SEPP) exception to apply for premature distributions from a retirement plan, payments must continue for _____ or until the participant is _____, whichever is longer.

   A. 5 years, age 59 ½
   B. 5 years, age 65
   C. 10 years, age 59 ½
   D. 10 years, age 65

19. Which of the following is/are correct regarding investment risk in a qualified retirement plan?

   (1) In a defined contribution plan, the employer bears the investment risk.
   (2) In a defined benefit plan, the employee bears the investment risk.

   A. (1) only
   B. (2) only
   C. None of the above
   D. All of the above

20. All but which of the following tests must be met in order for a retirement plan to receive favorable tax treatment as a qualified plan?

   A. Percentage test
   B. Ratio test
   C. Participation test
   D. Average benefit test

21. If an individual contributes more to an IRA than is permitted, the excess contribution is subject to a:

A. 5% excise tax.
B. 6% excise tax.
C. 10% excise tax.
D. 15% excise tax.

22. If a fully insured worker elects to receive social security retirement benefits early, which of the following is correct?

A. The benefit will be temporarily reduced until the worker reaches full retirement age.
B. The benefit will be temporarily reduced until the worker reaches age 70.
C. The benefit will be permanently reduced.
D. The benefit will be permanently reduced until the spouse reaches full retirement age.

23. An accounting firm has 125 employees. All employees are covered by the firm's defined benefit plan except for 70 junior associates. Has the minimum participation requirement been met for the defined benefit plan?

A. Yes, both parts of the 50/40 test have been met.
B. Yes, but only one part of the 50/40 test has been met.
C. No, neither part of the 50/40 test has been met.
D. No, only one part of the 50/40 test has been met and the plan must pass both tests.

24. All but which of the following are characteristics of a SEP IRA?

A. A SEP IRA is 100% owned by the participant.
B. A SEP IRA is 100% vested at all times.
C. Plan loans are permitted.
D. The contribution deadline to a SEP IRA is April 15 including extensions.

25. **Which of the following are considered fiduciaries?**

   (1) A plan administrator, including any third-party administrator that is used by the employer
   (2) A plan sponsor/employer, including its officers and/or directors
   (3) An investment advisor that renders advice to the plan for a fee or other compensation
   (4) A plan trustee

   A. (1) and (2) only
   B. (2) and (4) only
   C. (1), (2), and (3) only
   D. All of the above

26. **All qualified retirement plans must satisfy the reporting and disclosure requirements as specified by _____.**

   A. the PBGC
   B. ERISA
   C. the SEC
   D. the IRS

27. **For a SIMPLE plan, if an employer exceeds the maximum employee limit they are permitted to sponsor the plan for an additional _____ grace period.**

   A. 3 month
   B. 6 month
   C. 1 year
   D. 2 year

28. **When a qualified retirement plan is established, the summary plan description (SPD) must be provided to all plan participants within _____ days. For existing plans, the SPD must be provided to new plan participants within _____ days of becoming eligible for the plan.**

   A. 60, 90
   B. 90, 120
   C. 120, 90
   D. 90, 60

For questions 29-35, determine if the item listed is considered unrelated business taxable income (UBTI). Use only one answer per blank. Answers may be used more than once or not at all.

    A. Unrelated business taxable income (UBTI)
    B. <u>Not</u> unrelated business taxable income (UBTI)

29. _____ Dividends and interest

30. _____ Annuities

31. _____ Dividends from a stock purchased on margin

32. _____ Royalties

33. _____ Income from a non-real estate limited partnership

34. _____ Rents from real property (not debt financed)

35. _____ Gains from the sale or exchange of a capital asset

36. In order to maintain a SIMPLE plan, an employer may not have more than _____ employees.

    A. 25
    B. 50
    C. 75
    D. 100

37. In a defined benefit plan, if a participant's expected pension benefit is $2,000 per month, how much life insurance on the participant's life can the plan trustee apply for?

    A. $20,000
    B. $50,000
    C. $100,000
    D. $200,000

38. Which of the following is the penalty for a premature distribution from a qualified plan, 403b plan, IRA, or SEP?

A. 5%
B. 10%
C. 15%
D. Ordinary income tax rates

39. Amounts transferred from a qualified retirement plan to an IRA of a spouse or former spouse pursuant to a divorce decree are subject to which of the following penalties?

A. 0%
B. 10%
C. 15%
D. Ordinary income tax rates

40. In regards to the "21-and-1 rule", one year of service is defined as a calendar year, a plan year, or other consecutive _____ period during which _____ of service were completed by the employee.

A. 6-month, 2,000 hours
B. 12-month, 2,000 hours
C. 6-month, 1,000 hours
D. 12-month, 1,000 hours

41. Which of the following applies when a hardship withdrawal is taken from a 401k plan?

(1) A one-year blackout period exists on elective deferrals after a hardship withdrawal has been taken.
(2) The participant pays a 10% premature distribution penalty.
(3) The full distribution is taxed as ordinary income.
(4) The participant can recoup penalties and taxes paid by submitting a letter to the IRS showing the distribution qualified as a hardship withdrawal.

A. (1) and (2) only
B. (2) and (3) only
C. (1), (2), and (3) only
D. All of the above

42. Which of the following are characteristics of a SARSEP?

(1) A SARSEP allows for salary deferral contributions.
(2) A new SARSEP can be established if it is integrated with a 401k plan.
(3) A SARSEP may still be used in some businesses if it has been "grandfathered".
(4) SARSEPs must have been established prior to 1/1/2002 to be effective.

A. (1) and (3) only
B. (2) and (4) only
C. (1), (2), and (3) only
D. All of the above

For questions 43-53, determine if the fringe benefit listed is taxable or nontaxable. Use only one answer per blank. Answers may be used more than once or not at all.

A. Taxable fringe benefit
B. Nontaxable fringe benefit

43. ____ Use of employer-provided on-premise athletic facilities

44. ____ Meal and lodging provided to an employee for the employer's convenience

45. ____ Personal use of company car, airplane, or lodging

46. ____ No-additional-cost services to highly compensated employees only

47. ____ Working condition fringe benefits

48. ____ Employee achievement awards

49. ____ Country club dues paid by an employer on behalf of an employee

50. ____ De minimis fringe benefits

51. ____ Season tickets to a sporting event

52. ____ Business use of an employer-provided automobile

53. ____ Transportation benefits such as mass transit passes or free parking at the employer's place of business

54. There is an excise tax of _____ on the amount that should have been distributed from a retirement plan according to required minimum distribution rules but was not.

A. 25%
B. 50%
C. 75%
D. 100%

55. Hardship withdrawals from a 401k plan can only occur after a participant has demonstrated to the plan administrator which of the following?

A. The money will be paid back within five years.
B. The participant has an immediate and heavy financial need.
C. The money will be used for a first-time home purchase.
D. All of the above are correct.

56. Which of the following are characteristics of group term life insurance?

(1) Relatively low cost to the employer
(2) Requires a medical exam for employees to qualify for coverage
(3) Possible loss of coverage when the employee terminates employment
(4) Possible restriction on the amount of coverage that may be obtained by the employee

A. (1) and (4) only
B. (2) and (3) only
C. (1), (3), and (4) only
D. All of the above

57. All but which of the following are characteristics of an employee stock purchase plan (ESPP)?

A. The maximum discount permitted is 15% of the greater of the market price on the date the option is granted or the date the shares were purchased.
B. The plan must be offered to employees on a nondiscriminatory basis.
C. The maximum fair market value of stock an employee has the right to purchase cannot exceed $50,000 in any calendar year.
D. An ESPP allows a company to sell stock to employees at a discount from the market price.

58. For dependent group life insurance, the coverage on any dependent cannot exceed _____ of the coverage on the employee.

A. 25%
B. 50%
C. 100%
D. 200%

59. Which of the following is/are correct regarding executive group carve-out plans?

(1) Executive group carve-out plans provide individual, discriminatory benefits to selected employees.
(2) The cost of coverage is excluded from the executive's gross income.

A. (1) only
B. (2) only
C. None of the above
D. All of the above

60. Which of the following describes the tax treatment of premiums paid for group disability coverage?

A. The premiums paid are deductible by the employer as an ordinary and necessary business expense if benefits are paid to the employee.
B. The premiums paid are deductible by the employer as an ordinary and necessary business expense if benefits are paid to the employer.
C. The premiums paid are not deductible for coverage in excess of $50,000.
D. Group disability benefits attributed to employer paid premiums are not taxable to the employee.

61. Which of the following is/are correct regarding business overhead insurance?

(1) Business overhead insurance covers all ongoing business expenses during the time of an owner's disability, and may reimburse the owner/employee for his or her salary during that time.
(2) Business overhead insurance is designed to cover the ongoing expenses of a business if the owner becomes disabled.

A. (1) only
B. (2) only
C. None of the above
D. All of the above

62. Premiums paid for business overhead insurance are _____ to the owner and benefits received are _____.

A. non-deductible, taxable
B. deductible, non-taxable
C. non-deductible, non-taxable
D. deductible, taxable

63. All but which of the following are correct regarding nonqualified deferred compensation plans?

A. Provides executives with "customized" retirement plans
B. Avoids qualified plan nondiscrimination rules
C. Can provide retirement benefits in excess of qualified plan limits
D. Deferred amounts are subject to income tax when the benefit is promised

64. For COBRA continuation coverage, a terminating employee must pay the employer's share of insurance premiums, but the total cost may not exceed _____ of the overall cost of providing coverage to employees.

A. 50%
B. 100%
C. 102%
D. 104%

65. Which of the following is/are correct regarding the exercise price of incentive stock options (ISOs) and nonqualified stock options (NQSOs)?

(1) The exercise price of an ISO must be at least 50% of the stock's fair market value on the date the option is granted.
(2) NQSOs may be exercised at a discount to the stock's market price.

A. (1) only
B. (2) only
C. None of the above
D. All of the above

66. Which of the following groups may be excluded from participating in an employee stock purchase plan (ESPP)?

A. Employees working less than twenty hours per week
B. Employees with less than two years of service
C. Officers of the employer
D. All of the above may be excluded.

67. Which of the following is the tax consequence if an employer provides group prepaid legal services as a fringe benefit to an employee? Assume the employer pays for the entire benefit.

A. The fair market value of the benefit is excluded from the employee's gross income.
B. The fair market value of the benefit is included in the employee's gross income as W-2 income.
C. The fair market value of the benefit is included in the employee's gross income as passive income.
D. None of the above are correct.

68. Incentive stock options (ISOs) cannot be exercised more than _____ from the date of grant.

A. 5 years
B. 10 years
C. 15 years
D. 20 years

69. Which of the following is/are correct regarding **COBRA** continuation coverage?

(1) There is a penalty of $10/day/qualified beneficiary for failure to notify of the right to **COBRA** continuation coverage after a qualifying event such as termination of employment, change in work status, or death.

(2) **COBRA** continuation coverage may be conditioned upon evidence of insurability for a limited period of time.

A. (1) only
B. (2) only
C. None of the above
D. All of the above

70. Required minimum distributions (RMDs) from retirement plans are to begin when the participant turns age _____. If the first **RMD** is delayed until April 1 of the following year, the participant must take _____ before December 31 of that year. All subsequent **RMDs** must be taken by _____.

A. 70 ½, 1 distribution, December 31
B. 70 ½, 2 distributions, April 1
C. 70 ½, 2 distributions, December 31
D. 65, 1 distribution, April 1

71. Only the first _____ of ISO stock granted to an employee, which becomes exercisable for the first time during any single year, is entitled to favorable ISO treatment.

A. $50,000
B. $100,000
C. $250,000
D. $1,000,000

72. Which of the following are correct regarding ISOs and NQSOs?

   (1) ISOs may be granted to executives, key employees, or other groups of employees.
   (2) ISOs may be granted on a discriminatory basis.
   (3) NQSOs may be granted to executives, key employees, or other groups of employees.
   (4) NQSOs may be granted on a discriminatory basis.

   A. (1) and (3) only
   B. (2) and (4) only
   C. (1), (3), and (4) only
   D. All of the above

73. Premiums paid for group medical insurance are _____ to the employer and _____ to the employee.

   A. non-deductible, taxable
   B. deductible, non-taxable
   C. non-deductible, non-taxable
   D. deductible, taxable

74. The widow of a covered employee who requests COBRA continuation coverage is entitled to receive benefits for how many months?

   A. 9 months
   B. 18 months
   C. 29 months
   D. 36 months

75. Which of the following are required for an employee to defer taxes on a nonqualified deferred compensation plan?

   (1) The plan must be unfunded.
   (2) The plan must be funded.
   (3) The plan must be subject to substantial risk of forfeiture.
   (4) The plan must not be subject to substantial risk of forfeiture.

   A. (1) and (3) only
   B. (1) and (4) only
   C. (2) and (3) only
   D. All of the above will allow an employee to defer taxes.

76. In which of the following plans does an employee give up a specified portion of current compensation, and in return the employer promises to pay a benefit in the future equal to the amount deferred plus a predetermined rate of interest?

   A. Salary continuation plan
   B. Supplemental employee retirement plan
   C. Salary reduction plan
   D. Excess benefit plan

77. Which of the following are characteristics of restricted stock?

   (1) Must be issued to employees on a nondiscriminatory basis
   (2) Used as a form of incentive compensation for key employees
   (3) Subject to substantial risk of forfeiture so income (value of the shares) is not recognized at the time of the award
   (4) When no longer subject to risk of forfeiture, the value of the stock is recognized as ordinary income to the employee and is not deductible by the employer

   A. (2) and (3) only
   B. (2) and (4) only
   C. (1), (2), and (3) only
   D. All of the above

78. Which of the following is/are correct regarding excess benefit plans?

(1) Excess benefit plans make up for retirement benefits that were not permitted due to IRS limitations.

(2) Excess benefit plans are available to key employees only.

A. (1) only
B. (2) only
C. None of the above
D. All of the above

79. Which of the following doctrines states that an employee will be taxed on compensation that he or she has a right to receive on demand without any risk of forfeiture?

A. Accrual receipt doctrine
B. Constructive receipt doctrine
C. Earned income doctrine
D. Conditional receipt doctrine

80. Group paid-up life insurance consists of which of the following?

A. Increasing units of permanent insurance and decreasing units of term insurance
B. Increasing units of term insurance and decreasing units of permanent insurance
C. Increasing and decreasing units of permanent insurance
D. Increasing and decreasing units of term insurance

81. In which of the following circumstances does a substantial risk of forfeiture not exist?

A. Benefits paid are dependent upon an employee's continued employment for a specified period of time.
B. Benefits paid are dependent upon an employee following a non-compete agreement after leaving the employer.
C. Benefits paid are dependent upon death and disability.
D. Benefits paid are dependent upon an employee remaining available to provide consulting services following retirement.

82. Which of the following is/are correct regarding informally funded benefit plans?

(1) There is no taxation to the employee as long as the funds are subject to the company's creditors.
(2) The employee has no rights or secured interest in the assets.

A. (1) only
B. (2) only
C. None of the above
D. All of the above

83. A benefit plan is considered to be _____ if the deferred compensation is secured by property in which the employee has a beneficial interest.

A. funded
B. informally funded
C. conditionally funded
D. unfunded

84. Nonqualified stock options may be granted to which of the following groups?

(1) Employees
(2) Members of a board
(3) Independent contractors
(4) Consultants

A. (1) and (4) only
B. (1), (2), and (3) only
C. (2), (3), and (4) only
D. All of the above

85. Which of the following is a deferred compensation plan under which an employee receives the benefits of stock ownership without actually receiving company stock? Benefits are measured by the increase in value of the employer's stock.

A. Junior stock
B. Restricted stock
C. Phantom stock
D. Preferred stock

86. A salary reduction plan may also be referred to as which of the following?

A. Excess benefit plan
B. Supplemental employee retirement plan
C. Salary continuation plan
D. Pure deferred compensation plan

87. Which of the following is/are correct regarding profit sharing plans?

(1) Allocation formulas for profit sharing plans must be definite and predetermined.
(2) Contributions to a profit sharing plan must be allocated on a pro-rata basis.

A. (1) only
B. (2) only
C. None of the above
D. All of the above

88. Which of the following describes the tax consequences of nonqualified deferred compensation plans?

A. The employer is permitted an immediate deduction.
B. The employer is permitted a deduction in the year the employee is taxed.
C. The employer is not permitted a deduction because the plan is nonqualified.
D. None of the above are correct.

89. Employee enrollment in a qualified retirement plan may be postponed beyond one year of service if which of the following apply?

A. Contributions are made based on an age-weighted formula.
B. The employer agrees to match 100% of employee deferrals up to 10% of compensation.
C. Contributions are 100% immediately vested upon eligibility.
D. Key employees must wait longer than rank-and-file employees to enroll.

90. All but which of the following retirement plans are subject to the Pension Benefit Guaranty Corporation (PBGC)?

    A. Cash balance plan
    B. Target benefit plan
    C. Defined benefit plan
    D. All of the above are subject to the PBGC.

91. Which of the following is/are correct regarding profit sharing plans?

    (1) Company profits are required to make contributions to a profit sharing plan.
    (2) Profit sharing plans are best suited for companies with unstable cash flows.

    A. (1) only
    B. (2) only
    C. None of the above
    D. All of the above

92. In which of the following qualified retirement plans are the employees responsible for the investment risk?

    (1) Money purchase plans
    (2) Target benefit plans
    (3) Defined benefit plans
    (4) Cash balance plans

    A. (1) and (3) only
    B. (1) and (2) only
    C. (2) and (3) only
    D. (3) and (4) only

93. Under the social security system, the full retirement age for an insured worker born in the year 1960 or after is age _____.

    A. 63
    B. 65
    C. 66
    D. 67

94. The "50/40 test" for a defined benefit plan requires the plan must benefit the lesser of:

A. 50% of all employees or 40 employees.
B. 50 employees or 40% of all employees.
C. 50 highly compensated employees and 40% of all non-highly compensated employees.
D. 50% of all non-highly compensated employees and 40 highly compensated employees.

95. The excise tax for over contributing to an IRA will be imposed on a taxpayer:

A. for one year only.
B. for two years only.
C. for a period not to exceed five years.
D. each year the excess contribution remains in the account.

96. Which of the following is the contribution deadline to a SEP IRA?

A. December 31 of the year for which the contribution will apply
B. March 15 following the year for which the contribution will apply
C. April 15, excluding extensions, following the year for which the contribution will apply
D. April 15, including extensions, following the year for which the contribution will apply

97. Penalty-free distributions from an IRA for a first-time home purchase carry a lifetime maximum of _____.

A. $5,000
B. $10,000
C. $50,000
D. $100,000

98. Which of the following is/are correct regarding "substantial risk of forfeiture"?

(1) Substantial risk of forfeiture exists if a participant's right to compensation is not conditioned upon the future performance of substantial services.
(2) The risk of forfeiture must be real and substantial in order to defer taxes.

A. (1) only
B. (2) only
C. None of the above
D. All of the above

99. Which of the following is/are correct regarding phantom stock?

(1) Phantom stock dilutes existing company stock.
(2) Phantom stock is not actual stock, but is instead only a method of tracking the performance of company stock.

A. (1) only
B. (2) only
C. None of the above
D. All of the above

100. An employee will not be taxed on compensation if which of the following conditions are satisfied?

A. The employee elects to defer compensation under a written agreement before services are rendered.
B. The agreement between the employer and employee represents an unsecured promise to pay benefits.
C. The plan that will pay benefits to the employee is unfunded, or if funded, is subject to substantial risk of forfeiture.
D. All of the above are correct.

ANSWER KEY

1. D
In a SIMPLE IRA, early withdrawals are subject to a 25% penalty if the withdrawals are made during the first two years of plan participation.

2. C
Groups not covered under social security include federal employees hired before 1984, railroad employees, and newspaper delivery persons under age 18.

3. B
The two broad categories of defined contribution plans are profit sharing plans and pension plans.

4. D
Hardship withdrawals taken from a 401k plan before age 59 ½ typically require 2 years of plan participation.

5. D
Stock bonus plans protect company stock from hostile takeovers; provide a market for the owner's closely held shares of stock; provide a tax advantage to employees through net unrealized appreciation; and provide tax deductions while having no effect on cash flow.

6. A
A loan from a 401k plan cannot exceed $50,000 or 50% of the participant's vested benefit. If the vested amount is $10,000 or less, the entire amount can be made available for loan without regard to the 50% restriction.

7. B
The cost of employer-provided life insurance coverage up to $2,000 on dependents is excludible from income as a de minimis fringe benefit. The cost of coverage over the threshold is fully taxable to the employee.

8. C
Hardship withdrawals taken from a 401k plan are subject to a 10% premature distribution penalty.

9. B
Restricted stock is granted to an employee at no cost or at a bargain price with restrictions, such as the stock cannot be sold or disposed of before a specified period of time.

10. B
Defined benefit plans tend to favor older employees because the present value of the participant's promised benefit is greater the less time remaining until retirement.

11. B
Higher than expected turnover will result in a lower annual cost for a defined benefit plan.

12. A
Longer life expectancy will result in a higher annual cost for a defined benefit plan.

13. B
Higher than expected investment returns will result in a lower annual cost for a defined benefit plan.

14. B
Qualified domestic relations order (QDRO) rules apply to qualified retirement plans, 403b plans, and 457 plans. QDRO rules do not apply to nonqualified plans.

15. D
A benefit plan is considered to be unfunded if an employee has only the employer's promise to pay an amount sometime in the future out of future cash flow.

16. B
The two government agencies responsible for monitoring qualified retirement plan rules and eligibility are the IRS and the Department of Labor.

17. B
Employees must be eligible to participate in a 401k plan within 6 months after the later of attaining age 21 or completing 1 year of service.

18. A
For the substantially equal periodic payment (SEPP) exception to apply for premature distributions from a retirement plan, payments must continue for 5 years or until the participant is age 59 ½, whichever is longer.

19. C
In a defined contribution plan, the employee bears the investment risk. In a defined benefit plan, the employer bears the investment risk.

20. C

The three tests used to determine if a retirement plan will receive favorable tax treatment as a qualified plan are the percentage test, ratio test, and average benefit test.

21. B

If an individual contributes more to an IRA than is permitted, the excess contribution is subject to a 6% excise tax.

22. C

A fully insured worker may elect to receive social security retirement benefits early, but with a permanently reduced monthly benefit.

23. A

The minimum participation requirement has been satisfied because the plan covers at least the lesser of 50 employees ($125 - 70 = 55$) or 40% of all employees ($125 \times 40\% = 50$).

24. C

Plan loans are not permitted from SEP IRAs.

25. D

A fiduciary includes a plan administrator, including any third-party administrator that is used by the employer; a plan sponsor/employer, including its officers and/or directors; an investment advisor that renders advice to the plan for a fee or other compensation; and a plan trustee.

26. B

All qualified retirement plans must satisfy the reporting and disclosure requirements as specified by ERISA.

27. D

For a SIMPLE plan, if an employer exceeds the 100 employee limit they are permitted to sponsor the plan for an additional 2 year grace period.

28. C

When a qualified retirement plan is established, the summary plan description (SPD) must be provided to all plan participants within 120 days. For existing plans, the SPD must be provided to new plan participants within 90 days of becoming eligible for the plan.

29. B

Dividends and interest are <u>not</u> unrelated business taxable income.

30. B
Annuities are <u>not</u> unrelated business taxable income.

31. A
Dividends from a stock purchased on margin are unrelated business taxable income.

32. B
Royalties are <u>not</u> unrelated business taxable income.

33. A
Income from a non-real estate limited partnership is unrelated business taxable income.

34. B
Rents from real property (not debt financed) are <u>not</u> unrelated business taxable income.

35. B
Gains from the sale or exchange of a capital asset are <u>not</u> unrelated business taxable income.

36. D
In order to maintain a SIMPLE plan, an employer may not have more than 100 employees.

37. D
In a defined benefit plan, if a participant's expected pension benefit is $2,000 per month, the plan trustee can apply for $200,000 of insurance on the participant's life.

38. B
There is a 10% penalty on premature distributions from a qualified plan, 403b plan, IRA, or SEP.

39. A
Amounts transferred from a qualified retirement plan to an IRA of a spouse or former spouse pursuant to a divorce decree are not subject to a penalty, regardless of age.

40. D
In regards to the "21-and-1 rule", one year of service is defined as a calendar year, a plan year, or other consecutive 12-month period during which 1,000 hours of service were completed by the employee.

41. B
A six-month blackout period exists on elective deferrals after a hardship withdrawal has been taken from a 401k plan. The participant pays a 10% premature distribution penalty, and the full distribution is taxed as ordinary income.

42. A

SARSEPs must have been established prior to 1/1/1997 to be effective.

43. B

Use of employer-provided on-premise athletic facilities is a nontaxable fringe benefit.

44. B

Meal and lodging provided to an employee for the employer's convenience are nontaxable fringe benefits.

45. A

Personal use of a company car, airplane, or lodging is a taxable fringe benefit.

46. A

No-additional-cost services to highly compensated employees, if not available to rank-and-file employees, are taxable fringe benefits.

47. B

Working condition fringe benefits are nontaxable.

48. B

Employee achievement awards are nontaxable fringe benefits.

49. A

Country club dues paid by an employer on behalf of an employee are taxable fringe benefits.

50. B

De minimis fringe benefits are nontaxable.

51. A

Free tickets to entertainment or sporting events, other than occasional or de minimis benefits, are taxable.

52. B

Business use of an employer-provided automobile is a nontaxable fringe benefit.

53. B

Transportation benefits such as mass transit passes or free parking at the employer's place of business are nontaxable fringe benefits.

54. B
There is an excise tax of 50% on the amount that should have been distributed from a retirement plan according to required minimum distribution rules but was not.

55. B
Hardship withdrawals from a 401k plan can only occur after a participant has demonstrated to the plan administrator an immediate and heavy financial need.

56. C
A medical exam is not required for an employee to qualify for group term life insurance coverage.

57. C
The maximum fair market value of stock an employee has the right to purchase through an ESPP cannot exceed $25,000 in any calendar year.

58. B
For dependent group life insurance, the coverage on any dependent cannot exceed 50% of the coverage on the employee.

59. A
Executive group carve-out plans provide individual, discriminatory benefits to selected employees. The cost of coverage must be included in the executive's gross income and is deductible by the employer.

60. A
The premiums paid for group disability coverage are deductible by the employer as an ordinary and necessary business expense if benefits are paid to the employee.

61. B
Business overhead insurance covers all ongoing business expenses during the time of an owner's disability, but will not reimburse the owner/employee for his or her salary during that time.

62. D
Premiums paid for business overhead insurance are deductible to the owner and benefits received are taxable.

63. D
In a nonqualified deferred compensation plan, the employee is not required to pay tax on deferred amounts until the amounts are actually paid to the employee.

64. C

For COBRA continuation coverage, a terminating employee must pay the employer's share of insurance premiums, but the total cost may not exceed 102% of the overall cost of providing coverage to employees.

65. B

The exercise price of an ISO must be at least 100% of the stock's fair market value on the date the option is granted. Only NQSOs may be exercised at a discount to the stock's market price.

66. D

All of the groups listed may be excluded from participating in an employee stock purchase plan (ESPP).

67. B

If an employer provides group prepaid legal services as a fringe benefit to an employee, and the employer pays for the entire benefit, the fair market value of the benefit is included in the employee's gross income as W-2 income.

68. B

Incentive stock options (ISOs) cannot be exercised more than 10 years from the date of grant.

69. C

There is a penalty of $100/day/qualified beneficiary for failure to notify of the right to COBRA continuation coverage after a qualifying event such as termination of employment, change in work status, or death. COBRA continuation coverage cannot be conditioned upon evidence of insurability.

70. C

Required minimum distributions (RMDs) from retirement plans are to begin when the participant turns age 70 ½. If the first RMD is delayed until April 1 of the following year, the participant must take 2 distributions before December 31 of that year. All subsequent RMDs must be taken by December 31.

71. B

Only the first $100,000 of ISO stock granted to an employee, which becomes exercisable for the first time during any single year, is entitled to favorable ISO treatment.

72. D

ISOs and NQSOs may be granted to executives, key employees, or other groups of employees on a discriminatory basis.

73. B

Premiums paid for group medical insurance are deductible to the employer and non-taxable to the employee.

74. D

The widow of a covered employee who requests COBRA continuation coverage is entitled to receive benefits for 36 months.

75. A

For an employee to defer taxes on a nonqualified deferred compensation plan, the plan must be unfunded or subject to substantial risk of forfeiture.

76. C

In a salary reduction plan, an employee gives up a specified portion of current compensation, and in return the employer promises to pay a benefit in the future equal to the amount deferred plus a predetermined rate of interest.

77. A

Restricted stock may be issued to employees on a discriminatory basis. When no longer subject to risk of forfeiture, the value of the stock is recognized as ordinary income to the employee, and the employer is permitted to take a deduction at that time.

78. A

Excess benefit plans make up for retirement benefits that were not permitted due to IRS limitations.

79. B

According to the constructive receipt doctrine, an employee will be taxed on compensation that he or she has a right to receive on demand without any risk of forfeiture.

80. A

Group paid-up life insurance consists of increasing units of permanent insurance and decreasing units of term insurance.

81. C

Death and disability are not considered reasons for substantial risk of forfeiture.

82. D

In an informally funded benefit plan, there is no taxation to the employee as long as the funds are subject to the company's creditors. The employee has no rights or secured interest in the assets.

83. A

A benefit plan is considered to be funded if the deferred compensation is secured by property in which the employee has a beneficial interest.

84. D

Nonqualified stock options may be granted to employees, members of a board, independent contractors, and consultants.

85. C

Phantom stock is a deferred compensation plan under which the employee receives the benefits of stock ownership without actually receiving company stock. Benefits are measured by the increase in value of the employer's stock.

86. D

A salary reduction plan may also be referred to as a pure deferred compensation plan.

87. A

Although profit sharing contributions must be substantial and recurring, the allocation formula must be definite and predetermined. Contributions do not need to be allocated on a pro-rata basis.

88. B

For nonqualified deferred compensation plans, the employer is permitted to take a deduction in the year the employee is taxed.

89. C

Employee enrollment in a qualified retirement plan may be postponed beyond one year of service if contributions are 100% immediately vested upon eligibility.

90. B

Only defined benefit plans are subject to the PBGC. A target benefit plan is a type of defined contribution plan.

91. B

Profit sharing plans are best suited for companies with unstable cash flows because contributions must only be "substantial and recurring" and are not required annually.

92. B

The employee assumes the investment risk in a defined contribution plan. Money purchase plans and target benefit plans are types of defined contribution plans.

93. D

Under the social security system, the full retirement age for an insured worker born in the year 1960 or after is age 67.

94. B

The "50/40 test" for a defined benefit plan requires the plan must benefit the lesser of 50 employees or 40% of all employees.

95. D

The excise tax for over contributing to an IRA will be imposed on a taxpayer each year the excess contribution remains in the account.

96. D

The contribution deadline to a SEP IRA is April 15, including extensions, following the year for which the contribution will apply.

97. B

Penalty-free distributions from an IRA for a first-time home purchase carry a lifetime maximum of $10,000.

98. B

Substantial risk of forfeiture exists if a participant's right to compensation is conditioned upon the future performance of substantial services. The risk of forfeiture must be real and substantial in order to defer taxes.

99. B

Phantom stock is not actual stock, but is instead only a method of tracking the performance of company stock.

100. D

An employee will not be taxed on compensation if all three of the conditions listed are satisfied.

ESTATE PLANNING

QUESTIONS

1. When a person dies leaving a will, he or she is said to die _____. When a person dies without leaving a will, he or she dies _____.

   A. intestate, testate
   B. testate, noncupative
   C. intestate, noncupative
   D. testate, intestate

2. Which of the following are included in a decedent's gross estate?

   (1) Property owned by the decedent on his or her date of death
   (2) Interests in property in which the decedent retained the right of control or beneficial enjoyment as of the date of death
   (3) All property gifted within three years of the donor/decedent's death
   (4) Gift taxes paid on any gifts made within three years of the donor/decedent's death

   A. (1) and (2) only
   B. (1), (2), and (4) only
   C. (1), (3), and (4) only
   D. All of the above

3. All but which of the following are characteristics of a 2503(c) trust?

   A. Permits accumulation of income on behalf of a child
   B. Designed to use the gift tax annual exclusion
   C. Subject to kiddie tax rules
   D. Gift to a child under age 21 is not considered a gift of a future interest

For questions 4-8, determine how basis is treated at death for the following forms of property ownership. Use only one answer per blank. Answers may be used more than once or not at all.

  A. Step-up in basis for one-half property
  B. Full step-up in basis to the extent the property is included in the decedent's gross estate
  C. Full step-up in basis

4. ____ **JTWROS between spouses**

5. ____ **JTWROS between non-spouses**

6. ____ **Tenancy by entirety**

7. ____ **Tenancy in common**

8. ____ **Community property**

9. **All but which of the following are correct regarding probate?**

  A. Provides for clean title to a decedent's property
  B. The process by which a state or local court validates the will of a decedent
  C. Protects the decedent from an untimely filing of claims by his or her lifetime creditors
  D. May be either a public or private process depending on the wishes of the decedent

10. **Real property is probated according to the law of _____, meaning that out-of-state real property may undergo a separate or second probate.**

  A. situs
  B. ademption
  C. estoppel
  D. rescission

11. **Mark transfers property to an irrevocable trust, retaining the income from the trust for five years, at which time the trust property will be distributed to Erin. Which of the following will result if Mark dies during the five-year period?**

    A. All of the trust property will be included in Erin's gross estate at the fair market value the day the trust was created.
    B. All of the trust property will be included in Mark's gross estate at the fair market value the day the trust was created.
    C. All of the trust property will be included in Mark's gross estate at the date of death fair market value.
    D. All of the trust property will be included in Erin's gross estate at the date of death fair market value.

12. **In any single-life private annuity transaction, if the seller outlives his or her actuarial life expectancy, the purchaser will have paid _____ for the property. If the seller does not outlive his or her actuarial life expectancy, the _____ will have made a good financial deal.**

    A. too much, purchaser
    B. too little, seller
    C. too much, seller
    D. too little, purchaser

13. **Which of the following is/are correct regarding the amount of property that may be gifted between spouses?**

    (1) There is no limit on the amount of property that may be gifted tax-free between citizen spouses.
    (2) For non-citizen spouses, the annual amount of tax-free gifts is limited to $500,000 per year, or $1,000,000 for married couples.

    A. (1) only
    B. (2) only
    C. None of the above
    D. All of the above

For questions 14-21, match the type of will with the description that follows. Use only one answer per blank. Answers may be used more than once or not at all.

A. Holographic will
B. Noncupative will
C. Joint will
D. Mutual will
E. Living will
F. Simple will
G. Complex will
H. Pour-over will

14. _____ An oral will spoken by the testator.

15. _____ A testamentary device wherein the testator creates a trust, and decrees in the will that property in his or her estate at the time of death shall be distributed to the trustee of the trust.

16. _____ A single will that is signed by two testators.

17. _____ A will that does not include any estate tax planning measures and only distributes the testator's property outright to his or her spouse or other selected beneficiaries.

18. _____ A will that is handwritten entirely by the testator and is not witnessed by others.

19. _____ Each testator has his or her own will, but the content of the wills may deal with more than one testator.

20. _____ A legal document executed by an individual directing his or her physician to continue or discontinue life support measures.

21. _____ A will that includes estate tax planning measures.

22. All but which of the following are correct regarding completed gifts?

A. Gifts of a present interest are eligible for the gift tax annual exclusion.

B. Any consideration received by a donor will increase the value of the gift.

C. A gift made directly to an educational institution or medical care provider on behalf of another individual will be treated as a non-taxable gift.

D. Gifts may be split between spouses, thereby doubling the amount of property that may be gifted without gift tax liability to any number of donees.

23. Gift taxes paid are included in the gross estate of a donor for any taxable gifts made within _____ of death.

A. 6 months

B. 1 year

C. 2 years

D. 3 years

24. When making a taxable gift, a donor is required to complete which of the following IRS forms?

A. IRS Form 706

B. IRS Form 709

C. IRS Form 716

D. IRS Form 719

25. Lifetime taxable gifts are _____, meaning that prior taxable gifts must be _____ when computing the current taxable amount of gifts.

A. cumulative, excluded

B. cumulative, included

C. non-cumulative, excluded

D. non-cumulative, included

26. Which of the following is a state-imposed arrangement providing for the appointment of an individual responsible for managing the property of a ward?

A. Survivorship
B. Power of appointment
C. Guardianship
D. Conservatorship

27. A federal gift tax return must be filed if which of the following events occur?

A. The gifts from a donor to any single donee for a calendar year exceed the amount of the gift tax annual exclusion.
B. A gift of a future interest in property has been made for $5,000.
C. Spouses have split a $5,000 gift of individually owned property.
D. All of the above require a federal gift tax return to be filed.

28. When a decedent dies intestate and without family, the decedent's property will _____ to the state where he or she resided at the date of death.

A. reform
B. escheat
C. abate
D. estop

29. If the holder of a general power of appointment may only exercise the power with the consent of the grantor or an adverse third-party, which of the following is correct?

A. The general power of appointment will be non-taxable in the holder's gross estate.
B. The general power of appointment will be fully taxable in the holder's gross estate.
C. The general power of appointment will be partially taxable in the holder's gross estate.
D. None of the above are correct.

30. Property passing by contract includes which of the following?

A. Bank account subject to GSTT
B. Home titled JTWROS
C. Life insurance
D. Direct gift

31. In a year when the gift tax annual exclusion is $13,000, Phil and Sharon made a gift of $26,000 from their joint checking account to their adult daughter, Meredith. Which of the following is correct regarding the consequences of this gift?

   A. Filing a gift tax return is not necessary because the account was jointly owned.
   B. Filing a gift tax return is necessary because the gift was split between spouses.
   C. Filing a gift tax return is necessary because the full gift tax annual exclusion was used.
   D. Filing a gift tax return is necessary, although no gift taxes will be due.

32. Which of the following is an irrevocable trust created to pay for the supplemental needs of a disabled individual not covered by government assistance, while at the same time protecting those assets from governmental attachment?

   A. Special needs trust
   B. Contingent trust
   C. Standby trust
   D. Grantor trust

33. The federal estate tax return, _____, is due _____ after the date of the decedent's death, although an extension may be requested from the IRS and approved for reasonable cause.

   A. IRS Form 706, 6 months
   B. IRS Form 706, 9 months
   C. IRS Form 709, 6 months
   D. IRS Form 709, 9 months

34. Which of the following is/are correct regarding probate?

   (1) If a person dies testate, his or her property is subject to probate.
   (2) If a person dies intestate, his or her property avoids probate.

   A. (1) only
   B. (2) only
   C. None of the above
   D. All of the above

35. Which of the following is/are correct regarding gifts made to an educational institution or medical care provider?

   (1) Gifts made directly to an educational institution or medical care provider are not taxable gifts.
   (2) Gifts made first to a donee, who subsequently pays an educational institution or medical care provider, are subject to gift tax.

   A. (1) only
   B. (2) only
   C. None of the above
   D. All of the above

36. Bill establishes an irrevocable trust for the benefit of his two children and transfers $50,000 to the trustee of the trust. He gives his oldest child the right to lifetime income from the trust and, at the death of that child, the trust corpus will be distributed to the youngest child. Which of the following are correct regarding the transfer Bill has made?

   (1) Bill must split the gift of cash into a life estate and income interest.
   (2) The life estate of the first child qualifies for the gift tax annual exclusion.
   (3) The remainder interest of the second child does not qualify for the gift tax annual exclusion because it is a future interest gift.
   (4) Neither the life estate nor the remainder interest will qualify for the gift tax annual exclusion.

   A. (1) and (4) only
   B. (2) and (3) only
   C. (1), (2), and (3) only
   D. (1), (3), and (4) only

37. Which of the following is/are correct regarding simple and complex trusts?

   (1) A simple trust is required to pay out all of its income annually to trust beneficiaries and cannot distribute trust principal.
   (2) A complex trust may accumulate income or make distributions from trust principal.

   A. (1) only
   B. (2) only
   C. None of the above
   D. All of the above

38. Which of the following is a type of revocable trust in which the corpus consists of bank accounts and/or bank assets? At the grantor's death, the trust becomes irrevocable and avoids probate.

    A. Totten trust
    B. TOD trust
    C. POD trust
    D. Marital trust

39. Which of the following clauses will prohibit a beneficiary from assigning his or her interest in a trust to a creditor?

    A. Abatement clause
    B. Ademption clause
    C. Spendthrift clause
    D. Rescission clause

40. Which of the following trusts provides a surviving spouse with a lifetime interest in trust assets, and may include a right to invade principal on his or her behalf, limited to an ascertainable standard?

    A. Marital trust
    B. Credit shelter trust
    C. Crummey trust
    D. Estate trust

41. In which of the following trusts is the surviving spouse given a general power of appointment by the decedent spouse to distribute the decedent's property as the surviving spouse determines? Since the surviving spouse holds a general power of appointment, he or she may use trust assets to benefit him or herself directly.

    A. Marital trust
    B. Credit shelter trust
    C. QTIP trust
    D. Estate trust

42. Which of the following is correct if a grantor survives the trust term of a QPRT?

A. The fair market value of the home is included in the grantor's gross estate.
B. The home reverts back to the grantor.
C. The fair market value of the home is excluded from the grantor's gross estate.
D. The grantor is prohibited from living in the home, even if he or she pays rent at fair market value.

43. Which of the following is/are correct regarding CRATs and CRUTs?

(1) A CRUT may provide an inflation hedge or variable payments to a charitable income beneficiary.
(2) Additional contributions of property to a CRAT are permitted throughout the life of the trust.

A. (1) only
B. (2) only
C. None of the above
D. All of the above

44. The income tax deduction available when a _____ is created is equal to the total value of the property transferred to charity (the remainder interest) minus the present value of the income interest retained by the non-charitable beneficiary.

A. CLAT
B. CRUT
C. GRUT
D. GRIT

For questions 45-47, determine who is responsible for paying the GSTT due. Use only one answer per blank. Answers may be used more than once or not at all.

A. Direct skip
B. Taxable distribution
C. Taxable termination

45. _____ The trustee is responsible for paying the GSTT due.

46. _____ The transferor is responsible for paying the GSTT due.

47. _____ The transferee is responsible for paying the GSTT due.

48. In a _____, the donor transfers income-producing property to a reversionary trust and directs that trust income be transferred to a qualified charity initially for a period of time not to exceed twenty years.

A. charitable remainder trust
B. charitable lead trust
C. grantor retained trust
D. pooled income fund

49. All but which of the following are correct regarding pooled income funds?

A. A pooled income fund is generally created and maintained by a public charity, such as a private or public higher education institution or a not-for-profit hospital.
B. In a pooled income fund, the donor's gifted property is commingled with property transferred by other donors.
C. A benefit of a pooled income fund is that it can invest in tax-exempt securities.
D. Additional contributions of property are permitted into a pooled income fund.

50. Which of the following is not an incident of ownership in a life insurance policy?

A. The ability to change the beneficiary of the policy.
B. The ability to make premium payments on the policy.
C. The ability to surrender or cancel the policy.
D. The ability to pledge the policy for a loan.

51. Steve is the insured of a $2 million life insurance policy. He names his wife, Maria, as the owner of the policy and his adult child, Paul, as the beneficiary. Which of the following will occur at Steve's death?

A. At Steve's death, he will make an indirect gift of $2 million from his policy to Paul.
B. At Steve's death, the policy death benefits will be paid to Maria and no gift will occur.
C. At Steve's death, Maria will make an indirect gift of $2 million from Steve's policy to Paul.
D. At Steve's death, the policy death benefits will be paid to Paul and no gift will occur.

52. The death proceeds of a life insurance policy are included in the decedent's gross estate if which of the following occur?

A. The decedent maintained incidents of ownership in the policy at his or her date of death.
B. The death proceeds are payable to the decedent's estate.
C. The "three year rule" is triggered.
D. All of the above are correct.

53. Which of the following are valuation discounts for estate tax purposes?

(1) Minority interest discount
(2) Lack of marketability discount
(3) Non-voting discount
(4) Blockage discount

A. (1) and (3) only
B. (1), (2), and (4) only
C. (2), (3), and (4) only
D. All of the above

54. The fair market value of publicly traded stock, as included in the decedent/owner's gross estate, is determined by:

A. the closing price on the next to last trading day.
B. the mean between the highest and lowest quoted selling price on the applicable valuation date.
C. the closing price on the final trading day.
D. the opening price on the final trading day.

55. Which of the following is/are correct regarding self-canceling installment notes (SCINs)?

(1) A SCIN cancels the obligation of the buyer to make any remaining payments to the seller, if the seller dies.
(2) The buyer of a SCIN will receive a discount for the self-canceling feature of the note.

A. (1) only
B. (2) only
C. None of the above
D. All of the above

56. All but which of the following are correct regarding private annuities?

A. There is no includible value of remaining annuity payments in the decedent/annuitant's gross estate.

B. A private annuity provides lifetime income to the annuitant.

C. The annuity contract must be secured, and the purchaser is permitted an income tax deduction for any annuity payments that are made.

D. All of the above are correct regarding private annuities.

57. A skip person for GSTT purposes is an unrelated individual that is younger than the transferor by _____ or more.

A. 27.5 years

B. 32.5 years

C. 35.5 years

D. 37.5 years

58. Which of the following is not a triggering event that results in the application of GSTT?

A. Direct skip

B. Indirect skip

C. Taxable distribution

D. Taxable termination

59. To qualify for the Section 2032A "special-use valuation", the net value of real and personal property used in a family farming operation must be at least _____ of the adjusted value of the decedent's gross estate.

A. 25%

B. 35%

C. 45%

D. 50%

60. Which of the following qualify as income in respect of a decedent (IRD)?

(1) Accrued rental income
(2) Stock dividends paid after the decedent's death
(3) Required minimum distributions taken after death from an IRA
(4) Deferred compensation

A. (1) and (3) only
B. (1), (2), and (4) only
C. (2), (3), and (4) only
D. All of the above

61. If the alternate valuation date is elected, the assets in a decedent's gross estate may be valued at their fair market value _____ after the date of death.

A. 3 months
B. 6 months
C. 9 months
D. 1 year

62. Which of the following is/are correct regarding the alternate valuation date?

(1) If the alternate valuation date is elected, it must be used on all assets, and not just those that have declined in value since the date of death.
(2) The alternate valuation date may be used when property included in the gross estate has increased in value after the decedent's death.

A. (1) only
B. (2) only
C. None of the above
D. All of the above

63. Which of the following is correct regarding a qualified disclaimer?

    A. The disclaimer may be a revocable refusal by the beneficiary to accept a decedent's property or interest in property.

    B. The disclaimer may be oral or in writing.

    C. The beneficiary must not have previously accepted any interest in the benefits from the property.

    D. If the decedent did not name a "taker in default" in his or her will, the disclaimant is permitted to make this decision.

64. The Section 6166 election permits a decedent's estate to defer the payment of estate taxes relating to his or her interest in a closely-held business until the end of _____ after death. Only interest on the taxes due is paid during the deferral period, with taxes then paid in _____ beginning after the deferral period.

    A. 2 years, 8 annual installments

    B. 2 years, 10 annual installments

    C. 4 years, 8 annual installments

    D. 4 years, 10 annual installments

65. To qualify for the Section 6166 election, a decedent's gross estate must include an interest in a closely-held business that exceeds _____ of the value of his or her adjusted gross estate.

    A. 25%

    B. 35%

    C. 45%

    D. 50%

66. Section 303 redemption treatment may be used for which of the following entities?

    (1) C Corp
    (2) S Corp
    (3) Sole proprietorship
    (4) Partnership

    A. (1) and (2) only

    B. (3) and (4) only

    C. (1), (2), and (4) only

    D. All of the above

67. A qualified disclaimer must be made within _____ after the later of the date on which the transfer creating the interest was made, or the day on which the individual disclaiming the interest attains age _____.

A. 6 months, 18
B. 6 months, 21
C. 9 months, 18
D. 9 months, 21

68. To qualify for the Section 2032A "special use valuation", the net value of real property used in a family farming operation must be at least _____ of the adjusted value of the decedent's gross estate.

A. 25%
B. 35%
C. 45%
D. 50%

69. Jim and Linda Smith have lived in a community property state all their married lives. They own a house that is registered only in Linda's name. If she dies, what will happen to the house?

A. The house will pass automatically to Jim.
B. The house will pass automatically to Linda's closest family member.
C. Linda's half will pass by will. Jim already owns half under community property laws.
D. The house will pass through Linda's will, and the entire house will go to Jim.

70. All but which of the following are included in a decedent's probate estate?

A. Tenancy in common interest
B. Life insurance payable to a deceased beneficiary
C. Property held as tenancy by entirety
D. Property owned outright in the decedent's name

71. When is a gift considered to be complete?

A. When the recipient has the right to possess and enjoy the property
B. When the donor reports the gift on his or her gift tax return
C. When the donor intends for the gift to be complete
D. When the donor relinquishes dominion and control of the property

72. Crummey powers are used to create _____ interests from what would otherwise be _____ interests.

A. future, present
B. present, future
C. complete, incomplete
D. incomplete, complete

73. Which of the following is/are correct regarding the generation skipping transfer tax?

(1) Generation skipping may be for two generations only, i.e. grandparent to grandchild.
(2) The generation skipping transfer tax is always paid by the donor.

A. (1) only
B. (2) only
C. None of the above
D. All of the above

74. Which of the following is/are correct regarding durable powers of attorney?

(1) A durable power of attorney survives the death of the principal.
(2) A durable power of attorney survives disability of both the principal and the agent.

A. (1) only
B. (2) only
C. None of the above
D. All of the above

75. Which of the following is/are correct regarding the generation skipping transfer tax?

   (1) Transfers for qualified medical and tuition payments are exempt from gift tax and GSTT.
   (2) Transfers to family members are not subject to GSTT.

   A. (1) only
   B. (2) only
   C. None of the above
   D. All of the above

76. In a joint tenancy between non-spouses, _____ of the property will be included in the gross estate of the decedent unless the survivor shows consideration furnished.

   A. 100%
   B. 50%
   C. 25%
   D. 0%

For questions 77-83, determine if the item listed is included in a decedent's gross estate. Use only one answer per blank. Answers may be used more than once or not at all.

   A. Included in the decedent's gross estate
   B. Excluded from the decedent's gross estate

77. _____ POD/TOD account with daughter as beneficiary

78. _____ Face value of a life insurance policy on the life of a decedent that is owned by a beneficiary for ten years

79. _____ A life insurance policy on a decedent that was purchased by an ILIT one year ago

80. _____ Gifts made within three years of death

81. _____ The decedent's half of joint tenancy property held with a spouse

82. _____ An unexercised general power of appointment held by a decedent

83. _____ A life insurance policy on a decedent that was transferred to an ILIT one year ago

84. Which of the following is the limit on direct charitable contributions at death?

    A. 25% of the decedent's gross estate
    B. 50% of the decedent's gross estate
    C. 75% of the decedent's gross estate
    D. There is no limit.

85. Which of the following is/are correct regarding probate?

    (1) A decedent's estate will pay more federal estate tax if assets pass through probate.
    (2) Probate is held only in the state where the decedent dies.

    A. (1) only
    B. (2) only
    C. None of the above
    D. All of the above

86. In a/an _____ ILIT, the only property included in the trust is a life insurance policy on the life of the grantor.

    A. funded
    B. unfunded
    C. refundable
    D. non-refundable

87. Which of the following are necessary parties to a trust?

    A. Trustee, beneficiary, administrator
    B. Executor, decedent, beneficiary
    C. Trustor, trustee, beneficiary
    D. There are no necessary parties to a trust.

For questions 88-92, determine how property held in the following forms of ownership is included in a decedent's gross estate. Use only one answer per blank. Answers may be used more than once or not at all.

A. Half the property is included in the gross estate of the decedent regardless of contribution
B. Full value of the property is included in the gross estate of the decedent unless the survivor shows consideration furnished
C. Fractional ownership of the property is included in the decedent's gross estate

88. _____ **JTWROS between spouses**

89. _____ **JTWROS between non-spouses**

90. _____ **Tenancy by entirety**

91. _____ **Tenancy in common**

92. _____ **Community property**

93. **All but which of the following are methods of avoiding probate?**

A. Transfer assets by operation of law
B. Transfer assets by contract
C. Transfer assets by trust
D. Transfer assets by will

94. **When making a taxable gift, the donor is required to file a gift tax return by which of the following dates?**

A. April 15, including extensions, following the year in which the donor made the gift.
B. April 15, excluding extensions, following the year in which the donor made the gift.
C. December 31 of the year in which the donor made the gift.
D. December 31 following the year in which the donor made the gift.

95. Which of the following strategies will avoid ancillary probate?

(1) Irrevocable trust
(2) Testamentary trust
(3) Revocable living trust
(4) Deed delivered to an escrow agent

A. (2) and (4) only
B. (1), (2), and (3) only
C. (1), (3), and (4) only
D. All of the above

96. Which of the following may cause a will to be considered invalid?

(1) The testator was influenced by another person.
(2) The testator did not have adequate mental capacity to execute a will.

A. (1) only
B. (2) only
C. None of the above
D. All of the above

97. Cliff gives stock worth a total of $40,000 in equal shares to his two daughters. Cliff's basis in the stock was $16,000. What is each daughter's basis in the stock they now own?

A. $40,000
B. $20,000
C. $16,000
D. $8,000

98. Which of the following is correct if a decedent's estate is non-taxable for any reason?

A. The alternate valuation date cannot be used.
B. The alternate valuation date can be used to increase the basis of inherited property.
C. The alternate valuation date can be used, but only if the assets have decreased in value.
D. None of the above are correct.

99. To modify or amend a will, a testator must execute which of the following?

A. Substitute
B. Amendment
C. Codicil
D. Provision

100. The marital and charitable deductions are subtracted from a decedent's _____ to arrive at the _____ when calculating the total estate tax due.

A. gross estate, adjusted gross estate
B. adjusted gross estate, taxable estate
C. tentative tax base, tentative tax
D. net estate tax, total estate tax

ANSWER KEY

1. D

When a person dies leaving a will, he or she is said to die testate. When a person dies without leaving a will, he or she dies intestate.

2. B

Property included in a decedent's gross estate includes property owned by the decedent on his or her date of death; interests in property in which the decedent retained the right of control or beneficial enjoyment as of the date of death; and gift taxes paid on any gifts made within three years of the donor/decedent's death.

3. C

A 2503(c) trust escapes kiddie tax rules and is taxed at the trust's tax bracket.

4. A

JTWROS between spouses: Step-up in basis for one-half property

5. B

JTWROS between non-spouses: Full step-up in basis to the extent the property is included in the decedent's gross estate

6. A

Tenancy by entirety: Step-up in basis for one-half property

7. C

Tenancy in common: Full step-up in basis

8. C

Community property: Full step-up in basis

9. D

Probate is the process by which a state or local court validates the will of a decedent. It provides for clean title to a decedent's property, and protects a decedent from an untimely filing of claims by his or her lifetime creditors. Probate is a public process.

10.A

Real property is probated according to the law of situs, meaning that out-of-state real property may undergo a separate or second probate.

11.C

If Mark dies during the five-year period, all of the trust property will be included in his gross estate at the date of death fair market value.

12.A

In any single-life private annuity transaction, if the seller outlives his or her actuarial life expectancy, the purchaser will have paid too much for the property. If the seller does not outlive his or her actuarial life expectancy, the purchaser will have made a good financial deal.

13.A

There is no limit on the amount of property that may be gifted tax-free between citizen spouses.

14.B

Noncupative will: An oral will spoken by the testator.

15.H

Pour-over will: A testamentary device wherein the testator creates a trust, and decrees in the will that property in his or her estate at the time of death shall be distributed to the trustee of the trust.

16.C

Joint will: A single will that is signed by two testators.

17.F

Simple will: A will that does not include any estate tax planning measures and only distributes the testator's property outright to his or her spouse or other selected beneficiaries.

18.A

Holographic will: A will that is handwritten entirely by the testator and is not witnessed by others.

19.D

Mutual will: Each testator has his or her own will, but the content of the wills may deal with more than one testator.

20.E

Living will: A legal document executed by an individual directing his or her physician to continue or discontinue life support measures.

21. G

Complex will: A will that includes estate tax planning measures.

22. B

Any consideration received by a donor will decrease the value of a gift.

23. D

Gift taxes paid are included in the gross estate of a donor for any taxable gifts made within 3 years of death. This is known as the "gross-up rule".

24. B

When making a taxable gift, a donor is required to complete IRS Form 709.

25. B

Lifetime taxable gifts are cumulative, meaning that prior taxable gifts must be included when computing the current taxable amount of gifts.

26. D

A conservatorship is a state-imposed arrangement providing for the appointment of an individual responsible for managing the property of a ward.

27. D

A federal gift tax return must be filed if any of the events listed occur.

28. B

When a decedent dies intestate and without family, the decedent's property will escheat (pass) to the state where he or she resided at the date of death.

29. A

If the holder of a general power of appointment may only exercise the power with the consent of the grantor or an adverse third-party, the general power of appointment will be non-taxable in the holder's gross estate.

30. C

Life insurance passes by contract at a decedent's death.

31. A

Because the gift was made from a joint account, filing a federal gift tax return indicating the consent of either spouse is not necessary.

32. A
A special needs trust is an irrevocable trust created to pay for the supplemental needs of a disabled individual not covered by government assistance, while at the same time protecting those assets from governmental attachment.

33. B
The federal estate tax return, IRS Form 706, is due 9 months after the date of the decedent's death, although an extension may be requested from the IRS and approved for reasonable cause.

34. A
If a person dies testate or intestate, his or her property will be subject to probate.

35. D
Gifts made directly to an educational institution or medical care provider are not taxable gifts. Gifts made first to a donee, who subsequently pays an educational institution or medical care provider, are subject to gift tax.

36. B
Bill must split the gift of cash into a life estate and remainder interest. The life estate of the first child qualifies for the gift tax annual exclusion. The remainder interest of the second child does not qualify for the gift tax annual exclusion because it is a future interest gift.

37. D
A simple trust is required to pay out all of its income annually to trust beneficiaries and cannot distribute trust principal. A complex trust may accumulate income or make distributions from trust principal.

38. A
A Totten trust is a type of revocable trust in which the corpus consists of bank accounts and/or bank assets. At the grantor's death, the trust becomes irrevocable and avoids probate.

39. C
A spendthrift clause prohibits a beneficiary from assigning his or her interest in a trust to a current or future creditor.

40. B
A credit shelter trust (B trust) provides a surviving spouse with a lifetime interest in trust assets, and may include a right to invade trust principal on his or her behalf, limited to an ascertainable standard.

41. A

In a marital trust (A trust), the surviving spouse is given a general power of appointment by the decedent spouse to distribute the decedent's property as the surviving spouse determines. Since the surviving spouse holds a general power of appointment, he or she may use trust assets to benefit him or herself directly.

42. C

If a grantor survives the trust term of a QPRT, the fair market value of the home is excluded from the grantor's gross estate.

43. C

A CRUT may provide an inflation hedge or variable payments to a non-charitable income beneficiary. Additional contributions of property to a CRUT are permitted throughout the life of the trust.

44. B

The income tax deduction available when a CRUT is created is equal to the total value of the property transferred to charity (the remainder interest) minus the present value of the income interest retained by the non-charitable beneficiary.

45. C

In a taxable termination, the trustee is responsible for paying the GSTT due.

46. A

In a direct skip, the transferor is responsible for paying the GSTT due.

47. B

In a taxable distribution, the transferee is responsible for paying the GSTT due.

48. B

In a charitable lead trust, a donor transfers income-producing property to a reversionary trust and directs that trust income be transferred to a qualified charity initially for a period of time not to exceed twenty years.

49. C

A pooled income fund cannot invest in tax-exempt securities.

50. B

The ability to make premium payments on a life insurance policy is not considered an incident of ownership.

51. C
At Steve's death, Maria will make an indirect gift of $2 million from Steve's policy to Paul.

52. D
All of the items listed will cause the death proceeds of a life insurance policy to be included in the decedent's gross estate.

53. B
Valuation discounts include the minority interest discount, lack of marketability discount, and blockage discount.

54. B
The fair market value of publicly traded stock, as included in the decedent/owner's gross estate, is determined by the mean between the highest and lowest quoted selling price on the applicable valuation date.

55. A
A SCIN cancels the obligation of the buyer to make any remaining payments to the seller, if the seller dies. The buyer of a SCIN will pay a premium for the self-canceling feature of the note.

56. C
A private annuity contract must be unsecured, and the purchaser is not permitted an income tax deduction for the annuity payments that are made.

57. D
A skip person for GSTT purposes is an unrelated individual that is younger than the transferor by 37.5 years or more.

58. B
Triggering events that will result in the application of GSTT are the direct skip, taxable distribution, and taxable termination.

59. D
To qualify for the Section 2032A "special use valuation", the net value of real and personal property used in a family farming operation must be at least 50% of the adjusted value of the decedent's gross estate.

60. D
All of the items listed qualify as income in respect of a decedent (IRD).

61. B

If the alternate valuation date is elected, the assets in a decedent's gross estate may be valued at their fair market value 6 months after the date of death.

62. A

If the alternate valuation date is elected, it must be used on all assets, and not just those that have declined in value since the date of death.

63. C

In order to make a qualified disclaimer, the beneficiary must not have previously accepted any interest in the benefits from the property.

64. D

The Section 6166 election permits a decedent's estate to defer the payment of estate taxes relating to his or her interest in a closely-held business until the end of 4 years after death. Only interest on the taxes due is paid during the deferral period, with taxes then paid in 10 annual installments beginning after the deferral period.

65. B

To qualify for the Section 6166 election, a decedent's gross estate must include an interest in a closely-held business that exceeds 35% of the value of his or her adjusted gross estate.

66. A

Section 303 redemption treatment may only be used for an incorporated closely held business, such as a C Corp or S corp.

67. D

A qualified disclaimer must be made within 9 months after the later of the date on which the transfer creating the interest was made, or the day on which the individual disclaiming the interest attains age 21.

68. A

To qualify for the Section 2032A "special use valuation", the net value of real property used in a family farming operation must be at least 25% of the adjusted value of the decedent's gross estate.

69. C

Unless the house was bought by Linda with money earned prior to marriage, or with gift or inheritance money, the house is community property. The question does not provide this information, and it cannot be assumed. Therefore, Linda's half of the house will pass by will. Jim already owns half of the house under community property laws.

70. C

Property held as tenancy by entirety is not subject to probate.

71. D

A gift is complete when the donor relinquishes dominion and control of the property.

72. B

Crummey powers are used to create present interests from what would otherwise be future interests.

73. C

Generation skipping may be for more than two generations. The GSTT may be paid by the recipient, the donor, or the trustee.

74. C

A durable power of attorney does not survive the death of a principal or the disability of an agent.

75. A

Transfers for qualified medical and tuition payments are exempt from gift tax and GSTT.

76. A

In a joint tenancy between non-spouses, 100% of the property will be included in the gross estate of the decedent unless the survivor shows consideration furnished.

77. A

A bank account with a POD/TOD designation is included in a decedent's gross estate.

78. B

The face value of a life insurance policy on the life of a decedent that has been owned by a beneficiary for ten years is excluded from the decedent's gross estate.

79. B

A life insurance policy on a decedent that was purchased by an ILIT one year ago is excluded the decedent's gross estate.

80. B

Gifts made within three years of death are excluded from a decedent's gross estate.

81. A

The decedent's half of joint tenancy property held with a spouse is included in the decedent's gross estate.

82. A

An unexercised general power of appointment held by a decedent is included in the decedent's gross estate.

83. A

A life insurance policy on a decedent that was transferred to an ILIT one year ago is included in the decedent's gross estate.

84. D

Direct charitable contributions can be made at death without limit.

85. C

The federal estate tax is not affected by probate, although administrative costs may be reduced if probate is avoided. Probate may be held in a state other than where the decedent died. This is known as ancillary probate.

86. B

In an unfunded ILIT, the only property included in the trust is a life insurance policy on the life of the grantor.

87. C

The necessary parties to a trust are the trustor, trustee, and beneficiary.

88. A

JTWROS between spouses: Half the property is included in the gross estate of the decedent regardless of contribution.

89. B

JTWROS between non-spouses: Full value of the property is included in the gross estate of the decedent unless the survivor shows consideration furnished.

90. A

Tenancy by entirety: Half the property is included in the gross estate of the decedent regardless of contribution.

91. C

Tenancy in common: Fractional ownership of the property is included in the decedent's gross estate.

92. A

Community property: Half the property is included in the gross estate of the decedent regardless of contribution.

93. D

Assets can avoid probate if they pass by law, by contract, or by trust. Assets that pass by will are subject to probate.

94. A

When making a taxable gift, the donor is required to file a gift tax return by April 15, including extensions, following the year in which the donor made the gift.

95. C

A testamentary trust does not avoid probate because it is created by the will. Therefore, any property passing through a testamentary trust must first pass through probate.

96. B

A will may be considered invalid if the testator did not act of his or her own free will, or if the testator did not have adequate mental capacity to execute a will.

97. D

There is no step-up in basis for lifetime gifts. $16,000 / 2 daughters = $8,000 basis for each daughter.

98. A

If a decedent's estate is non-taxable for any reason (for example, full use of the marital deduction) the alternate valuation date cannot be used.

99. C

To modify or amend a will, a testator must execute a codicil.

100. B

The marital and charitable deductions are subtracted from a decedent's adjusted gross estate to arrive at the taxable estate when calculating the total estate tax due.

COMPREHENSIVE EXAM 1

QUESTIONS

1. Interest earned from EE bonds may be excluded from gross income if proceeds are used to pay for which of the following?

   A. First-time home purchase
   B. Medical expenses exceeding 7.5% of income
   C. Qualified higher education expenses
   D. Tax bill owed to the IRS

2. Which of the following are included as part of the financial planning step "Implementing the financial plan"?

   (1) Identifying activities necessary for implementation
   (2) Selecting products and services
   (3) Referring to other professionals
   (4) Coordinating with other professionals

   A. (2) and (4) only
   B. (1), (2), and (3) only
   C. (1), (3), and (4) only
   D. All of the above

3. Which of the following is/are correct regarding alimony and child support payments?

   (1) Excess alimony payments that are subject to recapture are fully taxable to the recipient.
   (2) Child support payments that are required pursuant to a divorce decree are deductible by the payor.

   A. (1) only
   B. (2) only
   C. None of the above
   D. All of the above

4. A loan up to _____ may be taken from a qualified retirement plan even if it is greater than one-half the participant's vested benefits.

A. $5,000
B. $10,000
C. $15,000
D. $50,000

5. Employee retirement expectations in a defined benefit plan are based on which of the following assumptions?

(1) Mortality rate of active and non-active participants
(2) Disability rate of active and non-active participants
(3) Employee turnover
(4) Retirement age of employees

A. (1) and (2) only
B. (3) and (4) only
C. (1), (3), and (4) only
D. All of the above

6. A call is an option to _____ a specified number of shares of stock during a specified period at a specified price. A buyer of a call option expects the price of the underlying stock to _____.

A. buy, fall
B. sell, rise
C. buy, rise
D. sell, fall

7. Which of the following is/are correct regarding use of the marital deduction?

(1) Probate is required to take full advantage of the marital deduction.
(2) The marital deduction is phased out for estates in excess of $10 million.

A. (1) only
B. (2) only
C. None of the above
D. All of the above

8. The allowable discount for employer-provided services is limited to _____ of the price at which the employer offers the same services to non-employees.

A. 20%
B. 25%
C. 30%
D. 50%

9. Justin's son recently got his driver's license when he turned age 16. As a gift, Justin bought his son a 20-year-old used car with 200,000 miles on it, for a cost of $1,000. Justin purchased liability insurance, but no damage protection for the vehicle. Which method of risk management is Justin using to deal with any potential damage that may occur to the car?

A. Reduction
B. Transfer
C. Avoidance
D. Retention

10. As bond interest rates _____, duration _____.

A. increase, increases
B. decrease, increases
C. decrease, decreases
D. increase, is unaffected

11. Distributions from a 401k plan following separation from service after age _____ are not subject to the _____ premature distribution penalty.

A. 50, 10%
B. 50, 15%
C. 55, 10%
D. 55, 15%

12. Which of the following is an offering of shares to existing stockholders on a pro-rata basis?

    A. Private placement
    B. Tender offering
    C. Public offering
    D. Rights offering

13. Which of the following are characteristics of a 2503(b) trust?

    (1) The trustee has no discretion to accumulate income.
    (2) Income must be paid out at least annually to the beneficiary.
    (3) Trust property must be distributed at age 21.
    (4) It is difficult to avoid kiddie tax because trust income must be distributed at least annually.

    A. (1) and (3) only
    B. (2) and (4) only
    C. (1), (2), and (4) only
    D. (2), (3), and (4) only

14. Which of the following is/are correct regarding profit sharing plans?

    (1) Profit sharing plans favor older employees.
    (2) Profit sharing plans can be invested entirely in company stock.

    A. (1) only
    B. (2) only
    C. None of the above
    D. All of the above

15. An investment grade bond is one that is rated _____ or higher by Moody's. A high-yield bond is rated _____ or lower by Moody's.

    A. Baa, Ba
    B. Baa3, Ba1
    C. Baa+, Ba-
    D. Ba, Baa

16. Which of the following is the typical limit on the term of a loan from a qualified retirement plan?

    A. 1 year
    B. 2 years
    C. 5 years
    D. 10 years

17. Which of the following is the most authoritative and carries the highest precedential value in defending a client's tax position against the IRS?

    A. Treasury Regulation
    B. Revenue Procedure
    C. Revenue Ruling
    D. Technical Advice Memorandum

18. All but which of the following are correct regarding a bond's call provision?

    A. Protects the issuer from declines in interest rates
    B. May be included in a bond agreement
    C. Allows the debtor to pay off the debt after a specific period of time at a predetermined price
    D. Will cause the investor's required rate of return to be lower

19. For a qualified retirement plan to pass the ratio test, the percentage of non-highly compensated employees who benefit under the plan must be at least _____ of the percentage of highly compensated employees who benefit under the plan.

    A. 50%
    B. 60%
    C. 70%
    D. 75%

20. All but which of the following are correct regarding the National Association of Insurance Commissioners (NAIC)?

    A. The NAIC has legal power in property and casualty matters.
    B. The NAIC coordinates regulatory activities.
    C. NAIC members exchange information and ideas.
    D. All of the above are correct.

21. A CRUT is designed to permit payment of trust assets to a _____ with the remainder passing to a _____.

    A. charity, non-charitable beneficiary
    B. non-charitable beneficiary, charity
    C. charity, charitable beneficiary
    D. non-charity, non-charitable beneficiary

22. All but which of the following are characteristics of defined contribution plans?

    A. Employer contributions are defined
    B. Employee assumes the risk of investment performance
    C. Employer assumes the risk of pre-retirement inflation
    D. Benefits cannot be provided for past service

23. An investor buys 100 shares of ABC stock for $60 per share with an initial margin of 50% and a 30% maintenance margin. At what price will the investor receive a margin call?

    A. $41.75
    B. $42.85
    C. $43.65
    D. $44.40

24. An active participant for purposes of deducting traditional IRA contributions is an individual who actively participates in all but which of the following retirement plans?

    A. 403b plan
    B. 457 plan
    B. SEP
    C. SIMPLE

25. According to the Principle of _____, in the course of professional activities, a CFP® Board designee shall not engage in conduct involving dishonesty, fraud, deceit or misrepresentation, or knowingly make a false or misleading statement to a client, employer, employee, professional colleague, governmental or other regulatory body or official, or any other person or entity.

    A. Competence
    B. Fairness
    C. Professionalism
    D. Integrity

26. A cash balance plan is a _____ plan with features similar to a _____ plan.

    A. defined benefit, defined contribution
    B. defined contribution, defined benefit
    C. pension, profit sharing
    D. profit sharing, pension

27. An investor's portfolio has experienced returns of +8%, -7%, +6%, +3%, and -2% over the past five years. What is the portfolio's standard deviation rounded to the nearest whole number?

    A. 5
    B. 6
    C. 8
    D. 9

28. An individual qualifies for a penalty-free distribution from an IRA for a first-time home purchase if he or she has not owned a principal residence during the preceding _____.

    A. 6 months
    B. 2 years
    C. 3 years
    D. 4 years

For questions 29-33, match the method of risk management with the description that follows. Use only one answer per blank. Answers may be used more than once or not at all.

    A. Retention
    B. Transfer
    C. Diversification
    D. Reduction
    E. Avoidance

29. ____ If a loss occurs, it will be absorbed.

30. ____ When a loss is large enough that it cannot be retained, insurance is purchased.

31. ____ The process of spreading risk over several possibilities for loss.

32. ____ An attempt to reduce the chance a loss will occur.

33. ____ Effectively making changes so a loss cannot occur.

34. Which of the following accurately describes ESPPs, ISOs, and NQSOs?

    A. ESPPs must be offered to all employees who qualify on a nondiscriminatory basis.
    B. ISOs may not be offered to employees on a discriminatory basis.
    C. NQSOs must be offered to all employees who qualify on a nondiscriminatory basis.
    D. All of the above are correct.

35. Which of the following are prohibited investments in an IRA?

    (1) US minted gold coins
    (2) Antiques
    (3) US stamps
    (4) Art work

    A. (1) only
    B. (1), (2), and (4) only
    C. (2), (3), and (4) only
    D. All of the above

36. In a positively skewed distribution, the median return is _____ the mean return. In a negatively skewed distribution, the median return is _____ the mean return.

   A. equal to, less than
   B. greater than, equal to
   C. less than, greater than
   D. greater than, less than

37. With a _____, the non-charitable income beneficiary receives payment of a fixed annual sum of at least _____ of the initial fair market value of trust assets. There is no provision for a variable payment.

   A. CRAT, 5%
   B. CLAT, 10%
   C. GRAT, 10%
   D. CRUT, 5%

38. Which of the following is correct regarding a Coverdell Education Savings Account (ESA)?

   A. Private elementary school expenses are permitted to be paid from an ESA.
   B. The cost of school uniforms is not a permitted expense to be paid from an ESA.
   C. Secondary school expenses are not permitted to be paid from an ESA.
   D. The maximum annual contribution to an ESA is $5,000 if the donor is younger than age 50.

39. Which of the following are among the requirements for an employee to be considered a key employee?

   (1) 5% owner
   (2) 1% owner with compensation exceeding $105,000
   (3) An executive of the company with compensation exceeding $150,000
   (4) An officer of the company with compensation exceeding $160,000

   A. (2) and (3) only
   B. (1) and (4) only
   C. (1), (2), and (3) only
   D. (1), (2), and (4) only

40. According to the principles of behavioral finance, which term describes an investor's tendency to look for information that supports his or her previously established decision, even if that decision was imprudent? This tendency may explain why investors are slow to sell an underperforming stock.

A. Prospect bias
B. Hold bias
C. Confirmation bias
D. Expectation bias

41. In order to be eligible to make a traditional IRA contribution, a taxpayer must be younger than age _____ by the end of the taxable year.

A. 59 ½
B. 65
C. 70 ½
D. 71

For questions 42-49, determine if the item listed is included in the decedent's probate estate. Use only one answer per blank. Answers may be used more than once or not at all.

A. Included in the decedent's probate estate
B. Excluded from the decedent's probate estate

42. ____ Life insurance on the life of a decedent, beneficiary is alive

43. ____ Life insurance on the life of a decedent, beneficiary is alive but disclaims, no contingent beneficiary is named

44. ____ 401k balance, child is beneficiary

45. ____ Tenancy in common interest with spouse

46. ____ Tenancy in common interest with business partner

47. ____ Life insurance on the life of a child, decedent was owner

48. ____ Assets in a living trust

49. ____ POD/TOD account with nephew as beneficiary

50. A portfolio with a beta of 1.0 has _____ risk only.

A. non-systematic
B. systematic
C. diversifiable
D. zero

51. Which of the following is/are correct regarding the transferability of incentive stock options (ISOs) and nonqualified stock options (NQSOs)?

(1) ISOs are not transferable by an employee except upon death.
(2) NQSOs may be gifted to family members.

A. (1) only
B. (2) only
C. None of the above
D. All of the above

52. Any income retained by a personal service corporation (PSC) is taxed at a flat _____ rate instead of graduated corporate tax rates.

A. 15%
B. 25%
C. 35%
D. 45%

53. Regarding hazards and perils, which of the following is correct concerning the risk of smoking a cigar indoors?

(1) Smoking a cigar indoors is a hazard.
(2) Smoking a cigar indoors is a peril.
(3) A fire that results from smoking indoors is a hazard.
(4) A fire that results from smoking indoors is a peril.

A. (1) and (3) only
B. (1) and (4) only
C. (2) and (3) only
D. (3) and (4) only

54. To satisfy the requirements of the rule against perpetuities, an interest must vest within _____ after the death of a "life in being". This life is generally someone that is still alive at the creation of the trust.

   A. 7 years
   B. 19 years
   C. 21 years
   D. 37.5 years

55. Jack invested $6,000 today with the promise that he will receive $11,000 in 4 years. If interest is compounded weekly, what is the average annual rate of return Jack will earn?

   A. 9.48%
   B. 12.72%
   C. 13.99%
   D. 15.18%

56. Which of the following is/are correct regarding **COBRA** continuation coverage?

   (1) **COBRA** continuation coverage is provided to children of a covered employee due to the loss of dependent status because of age limitations or marriage.
   (2) **COBRA** continuation coverage must be identical to coverage provided to employees, apart from cost.

   A. (1) only
   B. (2) only
   C. None of the above
   D. All of the above

57. The **Black-Scholes** valuation model assumes call options are _____ (exercisable only at the expiration date) and not _____ (exercisable at any time before expiration).

   A. Asian, American
   B. Asian, European
   C. American, European
   D. European, American

58. A prenuptial agreement is intended to address which of the following issues?

A. Who will be responsible for child support payments
B. Who will receive custody of children born during marriage
C. Who will own assets brought to the marriage
D. Who will pay alimony, and in what amount

59. When must an insurable interest exist for life insurance?

A. At the time the policy is written
B. At the time the loss is claimed
C. At the time the policy is written and at the time the loss is claimed
D. An insurable interest is not required for life insurance.

60. Katie purchased a new condo for $160,000. She financed the condo at 6.5% compounded monthly for 30 years. What payment is Katie required to make at the end of each month?

A. $1,001.63
B. $1,008.29
C. $1,011.31
D. $1,086.28

For questions 61-64, match the liability term with the description that follows. Use only one answer per blank. Answers may be used more than once or not at all.

A. Negligence
B. Libel
C. Slander
D. Malpractice

61. ____ Verbal or spoken false information about an individual that damages his or her reputation.

62. ____ Causing a loss to another through professional negligence.

63. ____ Causing an unintentional loss due to failure to use reasonable care.

64. ____ Writing false information about an individual that damages his or her reputation.

65. If a transfer takes place that is subject to GSTT, the tax is imposed as a _____ at the maximum transfer tax rate for the year of the transfer. The tax is assessed _____ any gift and/or federal estate tax that otherwise applies.

A. flat tax, in lieu of
B. flat tax, in addition to
C. graduated tax, in lieu of
D. graduated tax, in addition to

66. If a disability policy assumes an insured is disabled if he or she suffers a loss of both feet, both hands, loss of sight, or loss of hearing, then the policy likely contains which of the following provisions?

A. Presumptive disability provision
B. Residual benefit provision
C. Cost of living provision
D. Waiver of premium provision

67. Nina purchased an antique clock for $700. She kept the clock for 4 years and then sold it for $1,200. What internal rate of return (IRR) did Nina earn on her investment?

A. 11.1%
B. 12.2%
C. 13.3%
D. 14.4%

68. Tax returns are selected for audit through a program known as the _____.

A. Discriminant Function System (DIF)
B. Return Correlation System (RCS)
C. Primary Audit System (PAS)
D. Differentiating Formula System (DIF)

69. If the alternate valuation date is elected, it must result in a/an _____ in the total value of a decedent's gross estate, and must result in a/an _____ in the amount of federal estate tax payable by the decedent's estate.

   A. increase, increase
   B. reduction, reduction
   C. increase, reduction
   D. reduction, increase

70. Which of the following is/are correct regarding the capital structure of closed-end mutual funds?

   (1) A closed-end mutual fund has a fixed number of shares that, after original issue, trade on the secondary market.
   (2) The price an investor pays when buying shares of a closed-end mutual fund is based on supply and demand.

   A. (1) only
   B. (2) only
   C. None of the above
   D. All of the above

71. Luke started manufacturing a new type of protective helmet that he sells at the local bike shop. He wants to protect himself from liability in case a customer sues due to a defect in the helmet. He contacts his insurance agent to purchase a liability policy. Which method of risk management is Luke using?

   A. Reduction
   B. Transfer
   C. Retention
   D. Diversification

72. What is the IRR of a bond with a current price of $945, an 8% coupon, and 2 years until maturity?

   A. 5.57%
   B. 8.00%
   C. 11.14%
   D. 16.00%

73. A qualified beneficiary has _____ following a qualifying event to elect **COBRA** continuation coverage.

A. 30 days
B. 60 days
C. 90 days
D. 180 days

For questions 74-79, match the tax doctrine with the description that follows. Use only one answer per blank. Answers may be used more than once or not at all.

A. Substance over form
B. Assignment of income
C. Step transaction
D. Hobby Loss
E. Sham transaction
F. Tax benefit rule

74. ____ There must be a profit motive in order for a loss to be deductible.

75. ____ A transaction that lacks business purpose and economic substance will be ignored for deductibility purposes.

76. ____ Income is taxed to the "tree" that grows the "fruit" even though it may be assigned to another individual or entity prior to receipt.

77. ____ Financial statements should reflect the financial reality of an entity rather than the transactions and events that underlie them.

78. ____ Tax is imposed based upon the ultimate reality of an entire series of transactions rather than each transaction individually.

79. ____ If a taxpayer recovers an amount that was deducted against tax in a previous year, the recovery must be included in income to the extent the deduction reduced the tax liability in the earlier year.

80. An ISO must be held for at least _____ after the option is exercised and for at least _____ after the option is granted.

    A. 6 months, 1 year
    B. 6 months, 2 years
    C. 1 year, 2 years
    D. 2 years, 1 year

81. Which of the following is correct regarding the concept of adverse selection?

    A. Adverse selection commonly occurs in individual policies rather than group policies.
    B. Adverse selection occurs when high risk individuals are permitted to purchase insurance without paying adequate premiums for the risk assumed.
    C. Adverse selection occurs when low risk individuals are permitted to purchase insurance without paying adequate premiums for the risk assumed.
    D. Adverse selection occurs when high risk individuals are permitted to purchase insurance while paying adequate premiums for the risk assumed.

82. According to the Principle of _____, a CFP® Board designee shall act in the interest of the client.

    A. Integrity
    B. Competence
    C. Diligence
    D. Objectivity

83. The maintenance margin percentage is currently _____ as established by Regulation T of the Federal Reserve Board.

    A. 25%
    B. 30%
    C. 40%
    D. 50%

84. Which of the following is/are correct regarding Crummey powers?

(1) Crummey powers are limited to the greater of $5,000 or 5% of the trust value.
(2) If a beneficiary dies while having a Crummey power, the value of the power will be included in the beneficiary's gross estate.

A. (1) only
B. (2) only
C. None of the above
D. All of the above

85. Which of the following is the penalty for filing a tax return but failing to pay taxes owed?

A. 75% of the underpayment
B. 5% of the unpaid tax per month, up to a maximum of 25%
C. 0.5% of the unpaid tax per month, up to a maximum of 25%
D. 20% of the underpayment

86. Which of the following is/are correct regarding the tax implications of ISOs and NQSOs at the time of grant?

(1) Upon the grant of an ISO, no tax due.
(2) Upon the grant of an NQSO, the employee must recognize income for tax purposes.

A. (1) only
B. (2) only
C. None of the above
D. All of the above

87. Medicare Part B covers which of the following categories?

(1) Physician's services
(2) Care in a hospice facility for the terminally ill
(3) Home health care services not requiring a hospital stay
(4) Diagnostic tests

A. (1) and (2) only
B. (2) and (3) only
C. (1), (2), and (3) only
D. (1), (3), and (4) only

88. The limit on a loan from a qualified retirement plan is _____ of the participant's vested account balance, not to exceed _____.

A. 50%, $10,000
B. 50%, $50,000
C. 75%, $10,000
D. 100%, $50,000

89. Which of the following are short-term, fixed-income securities that may be bought or sold in the open market at a market-determined price?

A. Call options
B. Negotiable CDs
C. Eurodollars
D. ADRs

90. Which of the following is/are correct regarding profit sharing plans?

(1) Contributions to a profit sharing plan may not be skewed to favor older employees.
(2) The allocation formula may discriminate in favor of highly compensated employees.

A. (1) only
B. (2) only
C. None of the above
D. All of the above

91. A power of appointment is _____ in nature if the holder can benefit herself, her estate, or her lifetime creditors.

    A. limited
    B. specific
    C. general
    D. private

92. Which of the following is the minimum age requirement to use the substantially equal period payment (SEPP) exception to the 10% premature distribution penalty from an IRA?

    A. Age 21
    B. Age 59 ½
    C. Age 65
    D. There is no minimum age requirement.

93. All but which of the following property may qualify for a like-kind exchange?

    (1) Personal use property
    (2) Stocks and bonds
    (3) Inventory
    (4) Partnership interest

    A. (1) and (2) only
    B. (1) and (3) only
    C. (2), (3), and (4) only
    D. None of the above qualify for a like-kind exchange.

For questions 94-96, determine how the insurance policy listed is valued for gift tax purposes. Use only one answer per blank. Answers may be used more than once or not at all.

    A. Existing life insurance policy
    B. Paid-up life insurance policy
    C. New life insurance policy purchased for another person

94. ____ The gift tax value is the policy's interpolated terminal reserve plus the unearned portion of the paid premium.

95. ____ The gift tax value is the replacement cost for a comparable policy with the same company.

96. ____ The gift tax value is the gross premium paid for the policy.

97. Which of the following is/are correct regarding **COBRA** continuation coverage?

(1) **COBRA** continuation coverage is provided to employees who have changed from full-time to part-time status.
(2) **COBRA** continuation coverage is provided to spouses and dependents of a covered employee due to the employee's death, divorce, legal separation, or eligibility for **Medicare.**

A. (1) only
B. (2) only
C. None of the above
D. All of the above

98. Which of the following are permitted investments in an IRA?

A. A mutual fund that invests exclusively in a silver mining stock
B. Gold coins minted in the US
C. A REIT
D. All of the above can be purchased in an IRA.

99. Which of the following is not a type of REIT?

A. Hybrid REIT
B. Commercial REIT
C. Mortgage REIT
D. Equity REIT

100. When including a **Crummey** power in a trust, the beneficiary is given a _____ power of appointment by reason of his or her ability to access the grantor's annual contribution without restriction.

   A. limited
   B. specific
   C. general
   D. private

101. Assume the next dividend for **XYZ** stock will be $3 per share and investors require a 12% rate of return to purchase the stock. If the dividend for **XYZ** stock increases by 4% each year, what price should the stock be selling for today?

   A. $22.50
   B. $27.50
   C. $32.50
   D. $37.50

102. Which of the following is/are correct regarding the objectives of **ERISA?**

   (1) **ERISA** establishes criteria for investment selection for qualified retirement plans.
   (2) **ERISA** establishes minimum funding, eligibility, coverage, and vesting requirements for qualified retirement plans.

   A. (1) only
   B. (2) only
   C. None of the above
   D. All of the above

103. Gordon is self-employed and operates a sole proprietorship. He pays his 16-year-old daughter an hourly wage of $12.50 to enter sales data into his business computer. Gordon's daughter will earn $2,450 this year. Which of the following is correct regarding the wage Gordon pays his daughter?

   A. Gordon must withhold FICA and FUTA taxes.
   B. Gordon has to match his daughter's FICA and FUTA taxes.
   C. Gordon is not required to withhold taxes.
   D. None of the above are correct.

104. _____ risk cannot be eliminated through diversification because it affects the entire market. _____ risk may be diversified away or avoided by not investing in stocks that exhibit the risk.

A. Non-systematic, Unsystematic
B. Unsystematic, Systematic
C. Systematic, Unsystematic
D. Total, Systematic

105. Which of the following is a characteristic of a rabbi trust?

A. Revocable trust set up by an employer to provide nonqualified deferred compensation to employees.
B. Funds contributed to a rabbi trust must be available to pay benefits to employees. The assets cannot revert back to the employer.
C. Funds contributed to a rabbi trust are not subject to the claims of the company's creditors in the event of a bankruptcy.
D. None of the above are correct.

106. Which of the following is not a skip person for GSTT purposes?

(1) The transferor's spouse or former spouse, regardless of age.
(2) A grandchild of the transferor, if the transferor's child is deceased at the time of transfer.

A. (1) only
B. (2) only
C. None of the above
D. All of the above

107. The annual fee paid to a physician or group of physicians by each participant in a health plan is known as _____.

A. subrogation
B. indemnity
C. capitation
D. superannuation

108. Employer-provided group term life insurance has which of the following characteristics?

    (1) The cost of up to $100,000 of coverage is tax-free to each employee.
    (2) An employer can deduct its contribution to a group life insurance plan even if it pays for $200,000 of coverage.

    A. (1) only
    B. (2) only
    C. None of the above
    D. All of the above

109. A net operating loss (NOL) can be carried back _____ years preceding the year of the actual loss, and carried forward _____ years following the year of the loss.

    A. 2, 5
    B. 2, 10
    C. 2, 20
    D. 5, 10

110. Which of the following is/are correct regarding supplemental executive retirement plans (SERPs)?

    (1) SERPs are similar to excess benefit plans because they can be established to replace retirement benefits not permitted due to IRS limitations.
    (2) SERPs can provide additional retirement benefits above a company's qualified retirement plan calculations.

    A. (1) only
    B. (2) only
    C. None of the above
    D. All of the above

111. Medicare Part A is funded by _____, and Medicare Part B is funded by _____.

    A. premiums, payroll taxes
    B. payroll taxes, premiums
    C. premiums, the Department of Labor
    D. the Department of Labor, payroll taxes

For questions 112-114, match the type of risk with the description that follows. Use only one answer per blank. Answers may be used more than once or not at all.

A. Business risk
B. Tax risk
C. Financial risk
D. Market risk
E. Credit risk
F. Country risk

112. _____ The risk associated with a company's decision to use debt as part of its capital structure.

113. _____ The possibility that a bond issuer will default.

114. _____ The risk inherent in company operations.

115. Which of the following are correct regarding ISOs and NQSOs?

(1) Unlike an ISO, an NQSO does not have to meet any specific holding period rules.
(2) Unlike an NQSO, an ISO does not have to meet any specific holding period rules.
(3) With an ISO, the employee incurs a taxable event at the time the option is exercised.
(4) With an NQSO, the employee incurs a taxable event at the time the option is exercised.

A. (1) and (3) only
B. (1) and (4) only
C. (2) and (3) only
D. (1), (3), and (4) only

116. To avoid the underpayment of tax penalty, a self-employed individual must make estimated payments that are equal to the lesser of _____ of the tax liability shown on the current year's tax return, or _____ of the tax liability shown on the previous year's tax return, if the taxpayer's AGI for last year was $150,000 or less.

A. 75%, 90%
B. 90%, 100%
C. 90%, 110%
D. 100%, 110%

117. **Which of the following is correct regarding the unified credit?**

    A. The credit must be used the first time federal gift tax or estate tax is due.
    B. The credit is elective and is not mandatory.
    C. A taxpayer has the right to pay tax in lieu of using the credit. Therefore, the credit may be preserved for future use.
    D. All of the above are correct.

118. **Which of the following are activity ratios?**

    (1) Inventory turnover ratio
    (2) Average collection period
    (3) Fixed asset turnover ratio
    (4) Debt-to-equity ratio

    A. (1) and (4) only
    B. (1), (2), and (3) only
    C. (2), (3), and (4) only
    D. All of the above

119. **Penalty-free distributions from an IRA for a first-time home purchase must be used within _____ of the money being withdrawn.**

    A. 30 days
    B. 60 days
    C. 90 days
    D. 120 days

120. **If a personal auto policy (PAP) has Part A liability coverage of $25,000/$50,000/$15,000, which of the following is correct?**

    A. There is $15,000 coverage for each person injured in an auto accident, with a maximum of $50,000 coverage for all injured parties.
    B. There is $50,000 coverage for property damage.
    C. There is $25,000 coverage for property damage per vehicle insured, with a maximum of $50,000 coverage for all vehicles.
    D. There is $25,000 coverage for each person injured in an auto accident, with a maximum of $50,000 coverage for all injured parties.

121. **All but which of the following are characteristics of a defined benefit plan?**

A. Participant benefits vary
B. Employer contributions vary
C. Employer assumes the investment risk
D. Favors older employees

122. **Which of the following must occur for a company to revoke its S Corp status?**

A. A simple majority of stockholders can elect to revoke S Corp status.
B. The board of directors must elect to revoke S Corp status.
C. Two-thirds of the stockholders must elect to revoke S Corp status.
D. The S Corp must file a tax return as if it were a C Corp, which will effectively revoke the S Corp status.

123. **A general power of appointment is limited to an ascertainable standard if the power can only be exercised for which of the following?**

A. The holder's health, education, maintenance, or general welfare
B. The holder's health, education, maintenance, or enjoyment
C. The holder's health, education, maintenance, or comfort
D. The holder's health, education, maintenance, or support

124. **Which of the following typically invest in high-quality, short-term investments such as T-Bills, commercial paper, and negotiable CDs? The underlying investments have an average maturity of 30 to 90 days.**

A. Treasury bonds
B. Commercial paper
C. Money market funds
D. CDs

125. Which of the following is an irrevocable tax-exempt trust that funds a variety of benefits and may be established either by a collective bargaining agreement or directly by an employer? Its purpose is to provide employee benefits such as life insurance, health insurance, and severance pay.

A. Section 125 plan
B. Secular trust
C. VEBA
D. Rabbi trust

For questions 126-128, match the power of attorney with the description that follows. Use only one answer per blank. Answers may be used more than once or not at all.

A. Durable power of attorney
B. Non-durable power of attorney
C. Springing power of attorney

126. _____ The agent's ability to act on behalf of the principal comes into effect in the event of the principal's incapacity.

127. _____ The agent's ability to act on behalf of the principal continues in the event of the principal's incapacity.

128. _____ The agent's ability to act on behalf of the principal stops in the event of the principal's incapacity.

129. A photographer can no longer afford to replace his expensive camera that is constantly being damaged on photo shoots. He decides to only edit photos rather than take pictures. Which method of risk management is the photographer using?

A. Transfer
B. Reduction
C. Avoidance
D. Retention

130. Which of the following retirement plans is not subject to required minimum distribution rules during a participant's lifetime?

    A. SEP
    B. Roth IRA
    C. Tax-sheltered annuity
    D. SIMPLE

131. A _____ is issued by a governmental body to finance a specific project. It is not backed by the full faith and credit of the issuing body.

    A. revenue bond
    B. general obligation bond
    C. private activity bond
    D. multi-purpose bond

132. Which of the following will result if a distribution is taken from a health savings account (HSA) by an individual under age 65, and the distribution is not used to pay for qualifying medical expenses?

    A. The distribution is subject to ordinary income tax only.
    B. The distribution is subject to ordinary income tax and a 10% penalty.
    C. The distribution is subject to ordinary income tax and a 15% penalty.
    D. None of the above are correct.

For questions 133-135, match the form of the efficient market hypothesis with the description that follows. Use only one answer per blank. Answers may be used more than once or not at all.

    A. Strong form
    B. Semi-strong form
    C. Weak form

133. ____ Historical price data is already reflected in the current stock price and there is no value in predicting future price changes. However, fundamental analysis may generate superior performance. Technical analysis will not produce superior results.

134. _____ All historical information and industry conditions are already reflected in stock prices. Neither technical nor fundamental analysis can produce superior results over time on a risk-adjusted basis. Possessing insider information may lead to achieving returns in excess of the market.

135. _____ All public and private information is already reflected in stock prices. Neither technical nor fundamental analysis can improve the efficiency of the market to determine prices. Possessing insider information is not a factor in outperforming the overall market.

136. Which of the following is/are correct regarding living trusts and testamentary trusts?

   (1) Living trusts come into existence only upon death.
   (2) Testamentary trusts come into existence when the will is signed.

   A. (1) only
   B. (2) only
   C. None of the above
   D. All of the above

137. Martin, an individual taxpayer, donated $40,000 to the United Way last year when his gross income was $76,000. This year, when his gross income is $80,000, he makes no donations to charity. Martin could deduct _____ last year and _____ this year.

   A. $20,000, $4,000
   B. $22,500, $17,500
   C. $32,000, $8000
   D. $38,000, $2,000

138. A participant in a SIMPLE plan may rollover his or her account balance into a traditional IRA or SEP _____. A SIMPLE to SIMPLE rollover is permitted _____.

   A. after 1 year, anytime
   B. anytime, after 1 year
   C. after 2 years, anytime
   D. anytime, after 2 years

139. Buying a _____ and selling a _____ are both bearish strategies.

    A. put, call
    B. put, put
    C. call, call
    D. call, put

140. An actuary is required to establish and/or administer which of the following retirement plans?

    A. Profit sharing plan
    B. Target benefit plan
    C. Money purchase plan
    D. None of the above require an actuary.

141. All but which of the following are correct regarding the principles of waiver and estoppel?

    A. Estoppel is an intentional giving up of a right.
    B. Waiver and estoppel relate to misrepresentation and concealment.
    C. Waiver and estoppel are not confined to insurance contracts.
    D. Estoppel prevents a person or organization from adopting a position, action, or attitude inconsistent with an earlier position if it would result in an injury to another person.

142. Which of the following entities impose the reporting and disclosure requirements for defined benefit plans?

    A. ERISA
    B. SEC
    C. PBGC
    D. IRS

143. Which of the following is/are correct regarding the alternate valuation date?

   (1) The alternate valuation date cannot be used for "wasting assets" or those that automatically decrease with the passage of time.
   (2) "Wasting assets" include annuities, leases, patents, and installment sales.

   A. (1) only
   B. (2) only
   C. None of the above
   D. All of the above

144. A Section 412i plan, sometimes known as a fully insured pension plan, is funded exclusively with which of the following?

   A. Mutual funds and annuity contracts
   B. Term life insurance and annuity contracts
   C. Term life insurance and cash value life insurance
   D. Cash value life insurance and annuity contracts

145. Which of the following is correct regarding the relationship between a bond's coupon and its duration?

   A. Higher coupon = lower duration = lower interest rate risk
   B. Higher coupon = higher duration = higher interest rate risk
   C. Higher coupon = lower duration = higher interest rate risk
   D. Higher coupon = higher duration = lower interest rate risk

146. Target benefit plans share which of the following characteristics with defined benefit plans?

   (1) Contributions are determined through at least one actuarial calculation.
   (2) Individual account balances are not used to record the financial status of each participant.

   A. (1) only
   B. (2) only
   C. None of the above
   D. All of the above

147. Richard (AGI of $120,000) has an investment interest expense of $12,000 from his margin account and has $8,000 of investment income. He paid his investment advisor $5,000 for investment advice this year. How much investment interest expense can Richard deduct?

    A. $5,000
    B. $5,400
    C. $6,400
    D. $12,000

148. In a defined benefit plan, an insurance benefit must not be greater than _____ the expected monthly retirement income benefit.

    A. 10 times
    B. 50 times
    C. 75 times
    D. 100 times

For questions 149-153, determine if the form of property ownership listed is subject to probate. Use only one answer per blank. Answers may be used more than once or not at all.

    A. Avoids probate
    B. Goes to probate

149. ____ JTWROS between spouses

150. ____ JTWROS between non-spouses

151. ____ Tenancy in common

152. ____ Tenancy by entirety

153. ____ Community property

154. Which of the following plans require immediate vesting?

A. Employer contributions to a 401k plan
B. Employer contributions to a SEP
C. Employer contributions to a money purchase plan
D. All of the above require immediate vesting.

155. Which of the following is a characteristic of a debenture bond?

A. Debenture bondholders have the same rights as general creditors.
B. Debenture bonds are secured bonds.
C. To account for the lower default risk, debenture bonds will have lower YTMs than secured bonds issued for the same term by the same issuer.
D. All of the above are characteristics of debenture bonds.

156. In order for a loan from a qualified retirement plan to not be considered a taxable distribution to an employee, the term of the loan must not exceed _____, unless the loan proceeds are used to acquire a principal residence for the employee.

A. 2 years
B. 3 years
C. 5 years
D. 10 years

157. Which of the following are common exclusions that apply to all forms of homeowners insurance policies?

(1) Riot
(2) Earth movement
(3) Windstorm
(4) Nuclear hazard

A. (1) and (3) only
B. (2) and (4) only
C. (1), (2), and (3) only
D. (2), (3), and (4) only

158. Which of the following are permitted distribution options from a qualified retirement plan?

(1) Lump sum distribution
(2) Direct trustee-to-trustee transfer
(3) Payment in the form of an annuity or other periodic payment option
(4) Rollover of funds from one qualified retirement plan to another

A. (1) and (3) only
B. (1), (2), and (4) only
C. (2), (3), and (4) only
D. All of the above

159. Which of the following trusts does not qualify for the unlimited marital deduction in the grantor's estate, and trust assets are not included in the gross estate of the surviving spouse?

A. Marital trust
B. Credit shelter trust
C. QTIP trust
D. Estate trust

160. American Depository Receipts (ADRs) have which of the following characteristics?

(1) Dividends paid from an ADR are first declared in the local currency.
(2) American Depository Receipts eliminate exchange rate risk.

A. (1) only
B. (2) only
C. None of the above
D. All of the above

161. In a defined contribution plan, the premiums paid for term, universal, or variable life insurance coverage cannot exceed _____ of the contributions made to the plan on the participant's behalf.

A. 10%
B. 25%
C. 50%
D. 100%

162. Intentional torts include which of the following?

(1) Libel and slander
(2) Malpractice
(3) Strict liability
(4) Product liability

A. (2) only
B. (1) and (3) only
C. (1), (3), and (4) only
D. All of the above

163. Which of the following is/are correct regarding phantom stock?

(1) Income is recognized on the date phantom stock is awarded.
(2) Upon exercise, the entire amount of phantom stock is subject to capital gains tax rates.

A. (1) only
B. (2) only
C. None of the above
D. All of the above

164. Which of the following entities determines the minimum margin requirement for investment accounts?

A. PBGC
B. SIPC
C. Federal Reserve
D. SEC

165. How are forfeitures treated in a defined benefit plan?

A. Forfeitures must be used to increase each participant's account balance.
B. Forfeitures must be used to reduce the employer's cost of the plan.
C. Forfeitures may be used to increase each participant's account balance or reduce the employer's cost of the plan.
D. Forfeitures cannot occur because each participant in a defined benefit plan is 100% vested at all times.

166. Which of the following is/are correct regarding ILITs?

    (1) ILIT premium payments are always present interest gifts that qualify for the gift tax annual exclusion.
    (2) In an ILIT with Crummey powers, the beneficiary of the trust who receives the Crummey withdrawal power cannot be the grantor of the trust.

    A. (1) only
    B. (2) only
    C. None of the above
    D. All of the above

167. In order for a loan from a qualified retirement plan to not be treated as a prohibited transaction, which of the following must apply?

    (1) The loan must be made available to non-highly compensated employees only.
    (2) The loan must be made in accordance with the plan documents.
    (3) The loan may be provided for a flat 2% interest rate.
    (4) The loan must be adequately secured.

    A. (1) and (3) only
    B. (2) and (4) only
    C. (1), (2), and (3) only
    D. All of the above

168. If interest rates _____ following a bond issue, a sinking-fund provision will allow the issuing company to reduce the interest rate risk of its bonds as it replaces a portion of the existing debt with _____ bonds.

    A. decline, higher yielding
    B. rise, higher yielding
    C. decline, lower yielding
    D. rise, lower yielding

169. Which of the following is required by the IRS if a taxpayer uses the substantially equal periodic payment (SEPP) exception to the 10% premature distribution penalty?

    A. The taxpayer must show proof of economic hardship.
    B. The taxpayer must show proof that payments will be used to pay for qualified medical or education expenses.
    C. The taxpayer must show proof that appropriate taxes will be withheld.
    D. None of the above are correct.

170. Which of the following is/are correct regarding generation skipping transfers?

    (1) A generation skipping transfer may only occur during a transferor's lifetime.
    (2) The gift tax annual exclusion may only be used to offset a lifetime generation skipping transfer.

    A. (1) only
    B. (2) only
    C. None of the above
    D. All of the above

171. Which of the following is/are correct regarding active participation status in retirement plans?

    (1) An employee who makes voluntary contributions to a 403b plan is not considered an active participant.
    (2) An employee who does not make voluntary contributions to a 457 plan, but receives forfeitures in a profit sharing plan, is not considered an active participant.

    A. (1) only
    B. (2) only
    C. None of the above
    D. All of the above

For questions 172-174, match the bond hedging strategy with the description that follows. Use only one answer per blank. Answers may be used more than once or not at all.

A. Bond ladder
B. Bond bullet
C. Bond barbell

172. _____ An investment strategy where both short-term and long-term bonds are purchased.

173. _____ An investment strategy where several non-callable bonds mature at the same time.

174. _____ An investment strategy where an equal amount of money is invested in a series of bonds with staggered maturity dates.

175. A fiduciary under the provisions of **ERISA** is an individual who meets which of the following criteria?

(1) Has discretionary authority or responsibility over plan administration
(2) Exercises discretionary authority over plan management
(3) Renders investment advice for a fee or other compensation
(4) Exercises authority or control over the disposition of plan assets

A. (1) and (3) only
B. (2) and (4) only
C. (1), (2), and (4) only
D. All of the above

176. Which of the following is/are correct regarding powers of attorney and powers of appointment?

(1) A power of attorney is a legal document created by an individual authorizing someone else to act on his or her behalf.
(2) A power of appointment is a power given to a donee allowing him or her to dispose of the donor's property by selecting one or more beneficiaries to receive the property.

A. (1) only
B. (2) only
C. None of the above
D. All of the above

177. Which of the following are profitability ratios?

(1) Operating profit margin
(2) Net profit margin
(3) Return on assets
(4) Return on equity

A. (3) and (4) only
B. (1), (2), and (3) only
C. (1), (3), and (4) only
D. All of the above

178. Which of the following is/are correct regarding insurance provided by the PBGC?

(1) The PBGC provides mandatory insurance for defined benefit plans.
(2) The PBGC insures all pension plans, but not profit sharing plans.

A. (1) only
B. (2) only
C. None of the above
D. All of the above

179. **Which of the following is/are correct regarding generation skipping transfers?**

    (1) **A taxable distribution occurs when a distribution is made to a skip person from a trust when a non-skip person still has an interest in the trust.**
    (2) **A skip person is a related individual one or more generations younger than the transferor.**

    A. (1) only
    B. (2) only
    C. None of the above
    D. All of the above

180. **Investment risk can be defined as which of the following?**

    A. The chance an investment's actual return will be greater or less than its expected return
    B. The chance an investment's actual return will equal its expected return
    C. The chance an investment's actual return will be less than its expected return
    D. None of the above are correct.

181. **A plan is top-heavy if more than _____ of total plan benefits are in favor of _____.**

    A. 60%, highly compensated employees
    B. 70%, highly compensated employees
    C. 60%, key employees
    D. 70%, key employees

182. **According to the Principle of _____, RIA or R.I.A. following a CFP® Board designee's name in advertising, letterhead, or business cards may be misleading and is not permitted.**

    A. Objectivity
    B. Professionalism
    C. Fairness
    D. Diligence

183. Which of the following is/are correct regarding the early withdrawal penalty from a SIMPLE 401k?

(1) Early withdrawals are subject to a 25% penalty if the withdrawals are made during the first two years of plan participation.
(2) After the initial two-year period, early withdrawals from a SIMPLE 401k are subject to a 15% penalty.

A. (1) only
B. (2) only
C. None of the above
D. All of the above

184. Which of the following is/are correct regarding the early withdrawal penalty from a SIMPLE IRA?

(1) Early withdrawals are subject to a 20% penalty if the withdrawals are made during the first two years of plan participation.
(2) After the initial two-year period, early withdrawals from a SIMPLE IRA are subject to a 10% penalty.

A. (1) only
B. (2) only
C. None of the above
D. All of the above

185. If a grantor would like to transfer a primary residence and a vacation home into a QPRT, which of the following is correct?

A. The grantor can transfer both homes into a single QPRT.
B. The grantor must create two separate QPRTs, one for each property.
C. The grantor is not permitted to execute more than one QPRT at the same time.
D. Only the vacation home can be transferred into a QPRT, a principal residence is ineligible for QPRT treatment.

186. Which of the following is/are correct regarding a rabbi trust?

   (1) The trust may include a bankruptcy trigger.
   (2) Corporate assets may be contributed to the trust.

   A. (1) only
   B. (2) only
   C. None of the above
   D. All of the above

187. Which of the following is correct regarding the installment sale method of accounting?

   A. A taxpayer must receive approval from the IRS before using the installment sale method of accounting.
   B. The installment sale method of accounting has been replaced by the cash and accrual methods, and is no longer available to taxpayers.
   C. If payments made under a contract occur in more than one year, the installment sale method of accounting is permitted but is not required.
   D. If payments made under a contract occur in more than one year, the installment sale method of accounting is mandatory unless the seller opts out of the treatment.

188. If a retiree would like to receive social security benefits 24 months early, by how much will his or her benefits be reduced?

   A. 13.33%
   B. 16.66%
   C. 20.00%
   D. 25.00%

189. Which of the following is/are correct regarding a QPRT?

    (1) A residence in a QPRT may be occupied by someone other than the grantor or a member of the grantor's family during the term of the trust.
    (2) A QPRT is revocable.

    A. (1) only
    B. (2) only
    C. None of the above
    D. All of the above

190. Treasury STRIPS are always issued at a _____.

    A. premium to par
    B. discount to par
    C. price equal to par
    D. price above or below par

191. If an employer maintains a SIMPLE plan, which of the following plans can it also have in operation at the same time?

    A. Qualified plan
    B. 403b plan
    C. SEP
    D. None of the above are correct.

192. A CRUT is designed to permit payment of a fixed percentage of trust assets as revalued _____.

    A. only once at inception
    B. annually
    C. every two years
    D. twice per year

193. Treasury inflation protected securities (TIPS) are indexed to the rate of inflation as measured by which of the following?

    A. Producer Price Index (PPI)
    B. Personal Consumption Expenditures Price Index (PCEPI)
    C. Implicit Price Deflator (IPD)
    D. Consumer Price Index (CPI)

194. An individual who is not an active participant in a qualified retirement plan can deduct his or her contribution to a traditional IRA:

    A. if his or her income is less than $66,000.
    B. if his or her income is less than $120,000.
    C. regardless of income.
    D. never.

195. Jim would like to receive the equivalent of $19,000 in today's dollars at the beginning of each year for the next 18 years. Assume that inflation will average 5%, and Jim can earn a 4% compound annual rate of return on his investments. What lump sum does Jim need to invest today in order to achieve his goal?

    A. $312,665.24
    B. $315,671.63
    C. $371,438.46
    D. $375,009.99

196. ABC, Inc. adopts a defined benefit plan with a permitted disparity of 21.00%. Given the permitted disparity, the excess percentage is _____.

    A. 21.00%
    B. 26.25%
    C. 42.00%
    D. 47.25%

197. Which of the following plans will most likely be subject to forfeiture for the misconduct or termination of an executive?

    A. Incentive stock options
    B. Restricted stock
    C. Nonqualified stock options
    D. Stock appreciation rights

198. Under the social security system, a currently insured worker is one that has earned _____ quarters of coverage during the previous _____ calendar quarters.

    A. 5, 10
    B. 6, 12
    C. 6, 13
    D. 10, 40

199. Which of the following assets are correctly ranked from most liquid to least liquid?

    (1) Real estate
    (2) Treasury bills
    (3) Limited partnership
    (4) High-grade corporate bonds

    A. 2, 1, 4, 3
    B. 4, 2, 3, 1
    C. 3, 1, 4, 2
    D. 2, 4, 1, 3

200. Which of the following is/are correct regarding active participation status in retirement plans?

    (1) An employee who receives no contributions or forfeitures in a profit sharing plan is not considered an active participant.
    (2) An employee contributing to a 457 plan is considered an active participant.

    A. (1) only
    B. (2) only
    C. None of the above
    D. All of the above

ANSWER KEY

1. C

Interest earned from EE bonds may be excluded from gross income if proceeds are used to pay for qualified higher education expenses.

2. D

Implementing a client's financial plan includes identifying activities necessary for implementation; selecting products and services; determining implementation responsibilities of the client and financial planner; referring to other professionals; and coordinating with other professionals.

3. C

Excess alimony payments that are subject to recapture are not taxable to the recipient. Child support payments are not deductible by the payor.

4. B

A loan up to $10,000 may be taken from a qualified retirement plan even if it is greater than one-half the participant's vested benefits.

5. B

Employee retirement expectations in a defined benefit plan are based on assumptions about the mortality rate of active participants, disability rate of active participants, employee turnover, and the retirement age of employees.

6. C

A call is an option to buy a specified number of shares of stock during a specified period at a specified price. A buyer of a call option expects the price of the underlying stock to rise.

7. C

Probate is not required to use the marital deduction. There is no marital deduction phase out.

8. A

The allowable discount for employer-provided services is limited to 20% of the price at which the employer offers the same services to non-employees.

9. D

By not purchasing damage protection for the car, Justin is retaining the risk.

10. B
As bond interest rates decrease, duration increases.

11. C
Distributions from a 401k plan following separation from service after age 55 are not subject to the 10% premature distribution penalty.

12. D
A rights offering is an offering of shares to existing stockholders on a pro-rata basis.

13. C
In a 2503(b) trust, the trust property does not have to be distributed at any specific age.

14. B
Profit sharing plans tend to favor younger employees. They are not limited in their investment in company stock.

15. B
An investment grade bond is one that is rated Baa3 or higher by Moody's. A high-yield bond is rated Ba1 or lower by Moody's.

16. C
The typical limit on the term of a loan from a qualified retirement plan is 5 years.

17. A
Treasury Regulations are considered the most authoritative and carry the highest precedential value in defending a client's tax position against the IRS.

18. D
If a bond is callable it will cause an investor's required rate of return to be higher.

19. C
For a qualified retirement plan to pass the ratio test, the percentage of non-highly compensated employees who benefit under the plan must be at least 70% of the percentage of highly compensated employees who benefit under the plan.

20. A
The National Association of Insurance Commissioners (NAIC) has no legal power.

21. B
A CRUT is designed to permit payment of trust assets to a non-charitable beneficiary with the remainder passing to charity.

22. C
In a defined contribution plan, the employee assumes the risk of pre-retirement inflation.

23. B
Step 1: 100 shares x $60 = $6,000
Step 2: $6,000 - $3,000 equity = $3,000 margin
Step 3: $3,000 / 0.70 = $4,285
Step 4: $4,285 / 100 shares = $42.85

24. B
An active participant for purposes of deducting traditional IRA contributions is an individual who actively participates in a qualified retirement plan, SEP, or SIMPLE. Participating in a 457 plan does not make an individual an active participant for purposes of deducting traditional IRA contributions.

25. D
According to the Principle of Integrity, in the course of professional activities, a CFP® Board designee shall not engage in conduct involving dishonesty, fraud, deceit or misrepresentation, or knowingly make a false or misleading statement to a client, employer, employee, professional colleague, governmental or other regulatory body or official, or any other person or entity.

26. A
A cash balance plan is a defined benefit plan with features similar to a defined contribution plan.

27. B
Keystrokes to calculate standard deviation using the HP 12c calculator:
8, Σ
7, CHS, Σ
6, Σ
3, Σ
2, CHS, Σ
Blue g, s
6.1074, round to 6

28. B
An individual qualifies for a penalty-free distribution from an IRA for a first-time home purchase if he or she has not owned a principal residence during the preceding 2 years.

29. A
By retaining risk, if a loss occurs it will be absorbed.

30. B
When a loss is large enough that it cannot be retained, the risk is transferred to an insurance company.

31. C
Diversification is the process of spreading risk over several possibilities for loss.

32. D
Reduction is an attempt to reduce the chance a loss will occur.

33. E
Avoidance is effectively making changes so a loss cannot occur.

34. A
ESPPs must be offered to all employees who qualify on a nondiscriminatory basis. ISOs and NQSOs may be offered to employees on a discriminatory basis.

35. C
Collectibles that are prohibited investments in IRAs include antiques, stamps, art work, rugs, metals, gems, stamps, and coins. There is an exception for US minted gold coins.

36. C
In a positively skewed distribution, the median return is less than the mean return. In a negatively skewed distribution, the median return is greater than the mean return.

37. A
With a CRAT, the non-charitable income beneficiary receives payment of a fixed annual sum of at least 5% of the initial fair market value of trust assets. There is no provision for a variable payment.

38. A
Money in a Coverdell Education Savings Account (ESA) may be used to pay private elementary and/ or secondary school expenses. The cost of school uniforms is a permitted expense to be paid from an ESA. The maximum contribution to an ESA is $2,000 per beneficiary per year.

39. B
A key employee is an employee who meets any of the following conditions:
(1) A 5% owner
(2) A 1% owner with compensation exceeding $150,000
(3) An officer of the company with compensation exceeding $160,000

40. C

Confirmation bias may explain why investors are slow to sell an underperforming stock. It describes an investor's tendency to look for information that supports his or her previously established decision, even if that decision was imprudent.

41. C

In order to be eligible to make a traditional IRA contribution, a taxpayer must be younger than age 70 ½ by the end of the taxable year.

42. B

Excluded from the decedent's probate estate

43. A

Included in the decedent's probate estate

44. B

Excluded from the decedent's probate estate

45. A

Included in the decedent's probate estate

46. A

Included in the decedent's probate estate

47. A

Included in the decedent's probate estate

48. B

Excluded from the decedent's probate estate

49. B

Excluded from the decedent's probate estate

50. B

A portfolio with a beta of 1.0 has systematic risk only. The portfolio will move in the exact direction as the overall market.

51. D

ISOs are not transferable by an employee except upon death. NQSOs may be gifted to family members.

52. C
Any income retained by a personal service corporation (PSC) is taxed at a flat 35% rate instead of graduated corporate tax rates.

53. B
Smoking a cigar indoors (hazard) increases the chance that a loss from a fire (peril) will occur.

54. C
To satisfy the requirements of the rule against perpetuities, an interest must vest within 21 years after the death of a "life in being". This life is generally someone that is still alive at the creation of the trust.

55. D
PV = -$6,000
n = 4 x 52 = 208
FV = $11,000
PMT = 0
i = ? = 0.2918 x 52 = 15.18

56. D
COBRA continuation coverage is provided to children of a covered employee due to the loss of dependent status because of age limitations or marriage. COBRA continuation coverage must be identical to coverage provided to employees, apart from cost.

57. D
The Black-Scholes valuation model assumes call options are European (exercisable only at the expiration date) and not American (exercisable at any time before expiration).

58. C
A prenuptial agreement is intended to address who will own assets brought to the marriage.

59. A
For life insurance, an insurable interest must only exist at the time the policy is written.

60. C
PV = -$160,000
n = 30 x 12 = 360
i = 6.5 / 12 = 0.5417
FV = 0
PMT = ? = $1,011.31

61. C

Slander is verbal or spoken false information about an individual that damages his or her reputation.

62. D

Malpractice is causing a loss to another through professional negligence.

63. A

Negligence is causing an unintentional loss due to failure to use reasonable care.

64. B

Libel is writing false information about an individual that damages his or her reputation.

65. B

If a transfer takes place that is subject to GSTT, the tax is imposed as a flat tax at the maximum transfer tax rate for the year of the transfer. The tax is assessed in addition to any gift and/or federal estate tax that otherwise applies.

66. A

A presumptive disability provision assumes an insured is fully disabled and eligible to receive benefits if he or she suffers a loss of both feet, both hands, loss of sight, or loss of hearing.

67. D

PV = -$700

n = 4

FV = $1,200

PMT = 0

i = ? = 14.4

68. A

Tax returns are selected for audit through a program known as the Discriminant Function System (DIF).

69. B

If the alternate valuation date is elected, it must result in a reduction in the total value of a decedent's gross estate, and must result in a reduction in the amount of federal estate tax payable by the decedent's estate.

70. D

A closed-end mutual fund has a fixed number of shares that, after original issue, trade on the secondary market. The price an investor pays when buying shares of a closed-end mutual fund is based on supply and demand.

71. B
By purchasing a liability policy, Luke is transferring risk to the insurance company.

72. C
PV = -$945
n = 2 x 2 = 4
PMT = $1,000 x 0.80 = $80. $80 / 2 = $40
FV = $1,000
i = ? = 5.5717 x 2 = 11.14%

73. B
A qualified beneficiary has 60 days following a qualifying event to elect COBRA continuation coverage.

74. D
Hobby loss: There must be a profit motive in order for a loss to be deductible.

75. E
Sham transaction: A transaction that lacks business purpose and economic substance will be ignored for deductibility purposes.

76. B
Assignment of income: Income is taxed to the "tree" that grows the "fruit" even though it may be assigned to another individual or entity prior to receipt.

77. A
Substance over form: Financial statements should reflect the financial reality of an entity rather than the transactions and events that underlie them.

78. C
Step transaction: Tax is imposed based upon the ultimate reality of an entire series of transactions rather than each transaction individually.

79. F
Tax benefit rule: If a taxpayer recovers an amount that was deducted against tax in a previous year, the recovery must be included in income to the extent the deduction reduced the tax liability in the earlier year.

80. C
An ISO must be held for at least 1 year after the option is exercised and for at least 2 years after the option is granted.

81. B

Adverse selection occurs when high risk individuals are permitted to purchase insurance without paying adequate premiums for the risk assumed.

82. D

According to the Principle of Objectivity, a CFP® Board designee shall act in the interest of the client.

83. A

The maintenance margin percentage is currently 25% as established by Regulation T of the Federal Reserve Board.

84. B

If a beneficiary dies while having a Crummey power, the value of the power will be included in the beneficiary's gross estate.

85. C

If a tax return has been filed but taxes have not been paid, the penalty is 0.5% of the unpaid tax per month, up to a maximum of 25%.

86. A

No tax is due upon the grant of an ISO or NQSO.

87. D

Medicare Part B covers physician's services, home health care services not requiring a hospital stay, diagnostic tests, and hospital outpatient services.

88. B

The limit on a loan from a qualified retirement plan is 50% of the participant's vested account balance, not to exceed $50,000.

89. B

Negotiable CDs are short-term, fixed-income securities that may be bought or sold in the open market at a market-determined price.

90. C

For a profit sharing plan, contributions may be skewed to favor older participants through methods such as age-weighting and cross-testing. The allocation formula cannot be discriminatory.

91. C

A power of appointment is general in nature if the holder can benefit herself, her estate, or her lifetime creditors.

92. D

The substantially equal periodic payment (SEPP) exception to the 10% premature distribution penalty has no minimum age requirement.

93. D

Non-qualifying property for a like-kind exchange includes personal use property, stocks, bonds, inventory, and partnership interests.

94. A

The gift tax value of an existing life insurance policy is the policy's interpolated terminal reserve plus the unearned portion of the paid premium.

95. B

The gift tax value of a paid-up life insurance policy is the replacement cost for a comparable policy with the same company.

96. C

The gift tax value of a new life insurance policy purchased for another person is the gross premium paid for the policy.

97. D

COBRA continuation coverage is provided to employees who have changed from full-time to part-time status. It is also provided to spouses and dependents of a covered employee due to the employee's death, divorce, legal separation, or eligibility for Medicare.

98. D

All of the items listed are permitted investments in an IRA.

99. B

The three types of REITs are equity REITs, mortgage REITs, and hybrid REITs.

100. C

When including a Crummey power in a trust, the beneficiary is given a general power of appointment by reason of his or her ability to access the grantor's annual contribution without restriction.

101. D

Value = $3 / (0.12 - 0.04)

Value = $3 / 0.08

Value = $37.50 per share

102. B
ERISA establishes minimum funding, eligibility, coverage, and vesting requirements for qualified retirement plans.

103. C
A child, under age 18, who is employed by a parent in an unincorporated business, does not have to pay social security taxes.

104. C
Systematic risk cannot be eliminated through diversification because it affects the entire market. Unsystematic risk may be diversified away or avoided by not investing in stocks that exhibit the risk.

105. B
A rabbi trust is an irrevocable trust set up by an employer to provide nonqualified deferred compensation to employees. Funds contributed to a rabbi trust must be available to pay benefits to employees, and may not revert back to the employer. Funds contributed to a rabbi trust are subject to the claims of the company's creditors in the event of a bankruptcy.

106. D
A transferor's spouse or former spouse, regardless of age, is not a skip person for GSTT purposes. A grandchild of a transferor is not a skip person if the transferor's child is deceased at the time of transfer.

107. C
The annual fee paid to a physician or group of physicians by each participant in a health plan is known as capitation.

108. B
Only the cost of up to $50,000 of group term life insurance is excludible from an employee's income. However, an employer can deduct its contribution to a group term life insurance plan regardless of the amount of coverage it provides.

109. C
A net operating loss (NOL) can be carried back 2 years preceding the year of the actual loss, and carried forward 20 years following the year of the loss.

110. D
SERPs are similar to excess benefit plans because they can be established to replace retirement benefits not permitted due to IRS limitations. SERPs can provide additional retirement benefits above a company's qualified retirement plan calculations.

111. B
Medicare Part A is funded by payroll taxes, and Medicare Part B is funded by premiums.

112. C
Financial risk is the risk associated with a company's decision to use debt as part of its capital structure.

113. E
Credit risk is the possibility that a bond issuer will default.

114. A
Business risk is the risk inherent in company operations.

115. B
Unlike an ISO, an NQSO does not have to meet any specific holding period rules. With an NQSO, the employee incurs a taxable event at the time the option is exercised.

116. B
To avoid the underpayment of tax penalty, a self-employed individual must make estimated payments that are equal to the lesser of 90% of the tax liability shown on the current year's tax return, or 100% of the tax liability shown on the previous year's tax return, if the taxpayer's AGI for last year was $150,000 or less.

117. A
The unified credit must be used the first time federal gift tax or estate tax is due.

118. B
The activity ratios are the inventory turnover ratio, average collection period, and fixed asset turnover ratio.

119. D
Penalty-free distributions from an IRA for a first-time home purchase must be used within 120 days of the money being withdrawn.

120. D
There is $25,000 coverage for each person injured in an auto accident, with a maximum of $50,000 coverage for all injured parties. There is $15,000 coverage for property damage.

121. A
Participant benefits are fixed in a defined benefit plan.

122. A

A simple majority of stockholders can elect to revoke S Corp status.

123. D

A general power of appointment is limited to an ascertainable standard if the power can only be exercised for the holder's health, education, maintenance, or support.

124. C

Money market funds typically invest in high-quality, short-term investments, such as T-Bills, commercial paper, and negotiable CDs. The underlying investments have an average maturity of 30 to 90 days.

125. C

A VEBA (Voluntary Employee Beneficiary Association) trust is an irrevocable tax-exempt trust that funds a variety of benefits, and may be established either by a collective bargaining agreement or directly by an employer. Its purpose is to provide employee benefits such as life insurance, health insurance, and severance pay.

126. C

With a springing power of attorney, the agent's ability to act on behalf of the principal comes into effect in the event of the principal's incapacity.

127. A

With a durable power of attorney, the agent's ability to act on behalf of the principal continues in the event of the principal's incapacity.

128. B

With a non-durable power of attorney, the agent's ability to act on behalf of the principal stops in the event of the principal's incapacity.

129. C

The photographer is avoiding the risk that damage will occur to his camera by no longer taking pictures.

130. B

The lifetime required minimum distribution rules do not apply to Roth IRAs.

131. A

A revenue bond is issued by a governmental body to finance a specific project. It is not backed by the full faith and credit of the issuing body. Instead, debts are repaid from revenue generated from the project that was financed.

132. B

Distributions from a health savings account (HSA) that are not used to pay for qualifying medical expenses are subject to income tax and a 10% penalty. The penalty is waived if the individual is age 65 or older.

133. C

According to the weak form of the efficient market hypothesis, historical price data is already reflected in the current stock price and there is no value in predicting future price changes. However, fundamental analysis may generate superior performance. Technical analysis will not produce superior results.

134. B

According to the semi-strong form of the efficient market hypothesis, all historical information and industry conditions are already reflected in stock prices. Neither technical nor fundamental analysis can produce superior results over time on a risk-adjusted basis. Possessing insider information may lead to achieving returns in excess of the market.

135. A

According to the strong form of the efficient market hypothesis, all public and private information is already reflected in stock prices. Neither technical nor fundamental analysis can improve the efficiency of the market to determine prices. Possessing insider information is not a factor in outperforming the overall market.

136. C

Living trusts come into existence when signed. Testamentary trusts come into existence when the provisions of the will dictate and the will is probated.

137. D

Cash donations to qualified public charities are limited to 50% of the taxpayer's adjusted gross income. The excess amount can be carried forward to future years.

138. C

A participant in a SIMPLE plan may rollover his or her account balance into a traditional IRA or SEP after 2 years. A SIMPLE to SIMPLE rollover is permitted anytime.

139. A

Buying a put and selling a call are both bearish strategies.

140. B

Target benefit plans require an actuarial calculation at the inception of the plan.

141. A
A waiver is an intentional giving up of a right.

142. A
ERISA imposes the reporting and disclosure requirements for defined benefit plans.

143. D
The alternate valuation date cannot be used for "wasting assets" or those that automatically decrease with the passage of time. "Wasting assets" include annuities, leases, patents, and installment sales.

144. D
A Section 412i plan, sometimes known as a "fully insured pension plan", is funded exclusively with cash value life insurance and annuity contracts.

145. A
Higher coupon = lower duration = lower interest rate risk

146. A
Contributions are determined through at least one actuarial calculation for both target benefit plans and defined benefit plans. Individual account balances are unknown in defined benefit plans. They are only known in defined contribution plans, such as target benefit plans.

147. B
Investment interest expense calculation:
Step 1: Identify the investment income: $8,000
Step 2: $5,000 (fees) - $2,400 (2% of AGI) = $2,600
Step 3: $8,000 - $2,600 = $5,400

148. D
In a defined benefit plan, an insurance benefit must not be greater than 100 times the expected monthly retirement income benefit.

149. A
JTWROS between spouses avoids probate.

150. A
JTWROS between non-spouses avoids probate.

151. B
Tenancy in common goes to probate.

152. A
Tenancy by entirety avoids probate.

153. B
Community property goes to probate.

154. B
Employer contributions to a SEP require immediate vesting. A 401k plan and money purchase plan may use alternate vesting schedules.

155. A
Debenture bonds are unsecured bonds. Debenture bondholders have the same rights as general creditors. To account for the higher default risk, debenture bonds will have higher YTMs than secured bonds issued for the same term by the same issuer.

156. C
In order for a loan from a qualified retirement plan to not be considered a taxable distribution to an employee, the term of the loan must not exceed 5 years, unless the loan proceeds are used to acquire a principal residence for the employee.

157. B
The common exclusions that apply to all forms of homeowners insurance policies are water damage, neglect, ordinance of law, earth movement, power failure, war, nuclear hazard, and intentional loss.

158. D
The permitted distribution options from a qualified retirement plan are:
(1) Lump sum distribution
(2) Direct trustee-to-trustee transfer
(3) Payment in the form of an annuity or other periodic payment option
(4) Rollover of funds from one qualified retirement plan to another

159. B
A credit shelter trust (B trust) does not qualify for the unlimited marital deduction in the grantor's estate. The trust assets are not included in the gross estate of the surviving spouse.

160. A
Dividends paid from an ADR are first declared in the local currency, so exchange rate risk will exist.

161. B
In a defined contribution plan, the premiums paid for term, universal, or variable life insurance coverage cannot exceed 25% of the contributions made to the plan on the participant's behalf.

162. D
Intentional torts include libel, slander, malpractice, strict liability, and product liability.

163. C
No income is recognized on the date phantom stock is awarded. Upon exercise, the entire amount of phantom stock is subject to ordinary income tax rates

164. C
The Federal Reserve determines the minimum margin requirement for investment accounts.

165. B
In a defined benefit plan, forfeitures must be used to reduce the employer's cost of the plan.

166. B
ILIT premium payments without Crummey powers are future interest gifts. In an ILIT with Crummey powers, the beneficiary of the trust who receives the Crummey power cannot be the grantor of the trust.

167. B
In order for a loan from a qualified retirement plan to not be treated as a prohibited transaction, the loan must be available to all participants; must be made in accordance with the plan documents; must be made at a reasonable interest rate; and must be adequately secured.

168. C
If interest rates decline following a bond issue, a sinking-fund provision will allow an issuing company to reduce the interest rate risk of its bonds as it replaces a portion of the existing debt with lower yielding bonds.

169. D
For the substantially equal periodic payment (SEPP) exception to the 10% premature distribution penalty, the IRS does not require a reason for taking withdrawals.

170. B
A generation skipping transfer may occur during lifetime or at the transferor's death. The gift tax annual exclusion may only be used to offset a lifetime generation skipping transfer.

171. C
An employee who makes voluntary contributions to a 403b plan is considered an active participant. An employee who does not make voluntary contributions to a 457 plan, but receives forfeitures in a profit sharing plan, is also considered an active participant.

172. C
A bond barbell is an investment strategy where both short-term and long-term bonds are purchased.

173. B
A bond bullet is an investment strategy where several non-callable bonds mature at the same time.

174. A
A bond ladder is an investment strategy where an equal amount of money is invested in a series of bonds with staggered maturity dates.

175. D
A fiduciary under the provisions of ERISA is an individual that has discretionary authority or responsibility over plan administration; exercises discretionary authority over plan management; renders investment advice for a fee or other compensation; or exercises authority or control over the disposition of plan assets.

176. D
A power of attorney is a legal document created by an individual authorizing someone else to act on his or her behalf. A power of appointment is a power given to a donee allowing him or her to dispose of the donor's property by selecting one or more beneficiaries to receive the property.

177. D
The profitability ratios are the operating profit margin, net profit margin, return on assets, and return on equity.

178. A
The PBGC (Pension Benefit Guaranty Corporation) provides mandatory insurance for defined benefit plans only. It does not insure all pension plans, because some pension plans are defined contribution plans.

179. A
A taxable distribution occurs when a distribution is made to a skip person from a trust when a non-skip person still has an interest in the trust. A skip person for GSTT purposes is a related individual two or more generations younger than the transferor.

180. C
Investment risk is the chance an investment's actual return will be less than its expected return.

181. C
A plan is top-heavy if more than 60% of total plan benefits are in favor of key employees.

182. B

According to the Principle of Professionalism, RIA or R.I.A. following a CFP® Board designee's name in advertising, letterhead, or business cards may be misleading and is not permitted.

183. C

The 25% penalty for early withdrawals does not apply to SIMPLE 401ks. It only applies to SIMPLE IRAs. For a SIMPLE 401k, the early withdrawal penalty is always 10%.

184. B

Early withdrawals from a SIMPLE IRA are subject to a 25% penalty if the withdrawals are made during the first two years of plan participation. After the initial two-year period, the early withdrawal penalty is reduced to 10%.

185. B

A single QPRT may only contain one personal residence. If a grantor would like to transfer both a primary residence and a vacation home into a QPRT, then two separate trusts must be created.

186. B

A rabbi trust may not include a bankruptcy trigger because corporate executives could obtain benefits before creditors. The corporation may contribute corporate assets to the trust if the assets remain subject to the corporation's creditors.

187. D

If payments made under a contract occur in more than one year, the installment sale method of accounting is mandatory unless the seller opts out of the treatment.

188. A

The social security reduction is calculated as follows:
Step 1: 5 / 9 = 0.5556
Step 2: 0.5556 x .01 = 0.005556
Step 3: 0.005556 x 24 = 0.1333

189. C

A residence in a QPRT cannot be occupied by someone other than the grantor or a member of the grantor's family during the trust term. A QPRT is irrevocable.

190. B

Treasury STRIPS are always issued at a discount to par like zero-coupon bonds.

191. D
An employer cannot maintain any other qualified plan, 403b plan, or SEP at the same time it has a SIMPLE plan in operation.

192. B
A CRUT is designed to permit payment of a fixed percentage of trust assets as revalued annually.

193. D
Treasury inflation protected securities (TIPS) are indexed to the rate of inflation as measured by the Consumer Price Index (CPI).

194. C
A single individual who is not an active participant in a qualified retirement plan can deduct his or her contribution to a traditional IRA regardless of income.

195. C
Begin Mode
PMT = $19,000
n = 18
i = [(1.04 / 1.05) − 1] x 100 = -0.9524
FV = 0
PV = ? = $371,438.46

196. C
The permitted disparity in a defined benefit plan is the lesser of the base percentage of 21.00%, or 26.25%. The excess percentage is 21.00% + 21.00% = 42.00%.

197. B
Restricted stock is generally subject to forfeiture for the misconduct or termination of an executive.

198. C
Under the social security system, a currently insured worker is one that has earned 6 quarters of coverage during the previous 13 calendar quarters.

199. D
The assets ranked from most liquid to least liquid are Treasury bills, high-grade corporate bonds, real estate, and the limited partnership.

200. A
An employee who receives no contributions or forfeitures in a profit sharing plan is not considered an active participant.

COMPREHENSIVE EXAM 2

QUESTIONS

1. According to the Principle of _____, a CFP® Board designee's compensation shall be fair and reasonable.

   A. Integrity
   B. Fairness
   C. Confidentiality
   D. Professionalism

2. Assume an investor's portfolio has an actual realized return of 16%. The realized return of the S&P 500 for the same time period is 18% and the risk-free rate is 6%. The beta of the portfolio is 0.75. What is the portfolio's alpha?

   A. -0.02
   B. -0.01
   C. +0.01
   D. +0.02

3. Jane dies owning XYZ stock, which is thinly traded. The nearest trading dates for XYZ stock were two days before the valuation date and four days after the valuation date. The mean price of the stock two days before the valuation date was $8, and the mean price four days after the valuation date was $10. What is the reportable value of XYZ stock in Jane's gross estate?

   A. $8.00
   B. $8.67
   C. $9.00
   D. $9.67

4. Which of the following measures the thickness of the tail on a normal distribution chart of investment returns?

A. Poisson distribution
B. Skewness
C. Range
D. Kurtosis

5. According to the _____ clause, the primary beneficiary of a life insurance policy must survive the insured by a certain number of days in order to receive insurance proceeds. Otherwise the proceeds will be paid to the insured's contingent beneficiary.

A. simultaneous death
B. common disaster
C. statute of limitations
D. common death

6. Which of the following is correct regarding commercial paper?

A. Has a maturity of 270 days or less
B. Issued in denominations of $1,000 or more
C. Does not act as a viable substitute for short-term bank financing
D. Has less default risk than Treasury bills

7. Under the valuation rules of Section 2703, which of the following is required for a buy-sell agreement to be effective?

A. Must be a bona-fide business arrangement
B. Must not be a device to transfer property to a decedent's family member for less than full and adequate consideration
C. Must include terms that represent an arm's length transaction
D. All of the above are correct.

8. Which of the following is preferred by a risk-averse investor?

   A. High kurtosis
   B. Mid kurtosis
   C. Low kurtosis
   D. Kurtosis is insignificant.

9. Which of the following is/are correct regarding rabbi trusts?

   (1) A rabbi trust may contain an insolvency trigger. Therefore it can be used to protect executives in the event of employer bankruptcy.
   (2) A rabbi trust can protect executives in the event of a hostile takeover or merger.

   A. (1) only
   B. (2) only
   C. None of the above
   D. All of the above

10. Tony wants to purchase a new sailboat in 3 years. He expects to spend $15,000 for the boat. If he earns an annual compound rate of return of 8% on his investments, how much should he invest at the end of each year to achieve his goal?

   A. $4,278.24
   B. $4,620.50
   C. $4,930.91
   D. $5,110.45

11. A skip person for GSTT purposes is a related individual _____ below that of the transferor.

   A. one or more generations
   B. two or more generations
   C. 21 years
   D. 37.5 years

12. According to the misstatement of age clause found in life insurance policies, if it is discovered that an insured is older or younger than the age stated on his or her application, which of the following will result?

    A. The full death benefit will be paid if the misstatement of age was discovered after two years from the policy's inception.
    B. The death benefit will be adjusted to what the premiums paid would have purchased if based on the correct age.
    C. No death benefit will be paid and the insured may be sued for breach of contract.
    D. The death benefit may be lowered by a maximum of 25%.

13. The power to appoint assets to oneself that can be exercised only with the consent of an adverse third-party is considered which of the following?

    A. Special power of appointment
    B. General power of appointment
    C. Broad power of appointment
    D. Crummey power of appointment

14. Which of the following may be referred to as a hybrid security?

    A. Corporate bond
    B. Common stock
    C. Preferred stock
    D. REIT

15. Alimony payments are _____ by the payor and _____ to the recipient.

    A. non-deductible, non-taxable
    B. deductible, taxable
    C. taxable, deductible
    D. non-taxable, non-deductible

16. **For married couples, each spouse is entitled to receive a social security benefit based on the greater of his or her own retirement benefit, or _____ of the spouse's benefit.**

    A. 50%
    B. 66%
    C. 75%
    D. 100%

17. **How are the death benefits of a MEC taxed?**

    A. Taxed as ordinary income to the beneficiary
    B. Taxed at capital gains rates to the beneficiary
    C. Taxed partly as ordinary income and partly as capital gains
    D. Death benefits are treated the same as any non-MEC life insurance policy

18. **Higher inflation = _____ interest rates = _____ bond values**

    A. lower, lower
    B. higher, higher
    C. lower, higher
    D. higher, lower

19. **In order for an individual to qualify for Medicaid, he or she must meet which of the following tests?**

    A. The income test only
    B. The asset test only
    C. The income test and the asset test
    D. Neither test needs to be met.

20. **Which of the following provisions may prevent a life insurance policy from lapsing?**

    A. Reinstatement provision
    B. Contestable period provision
    C. Conversion provision
    D. Automatic premium loan provision

For questions 21-24, match the legislation with the description that follows. Use only one answer per blank. Answers may be used more than once or not at all.

    A. Securities Act of 1933
    B. Securities Act of 1934
    C. Investment Company Act of 1940
    D. SIPC of 1970

21. _____ **Regulates brokerage firms**

22. _____ **Regulates mutual funds**

23. _____ **Regulates existing securities**

24. _____ **Regulates new securities**

25. Vijay opened a college savings account when his son was born and deposited $4,000 into the account. Today the account has a value of $7,000. How old is Vijay's son if the deposit has been growing at an annual rate of 7% compounded annually?

    A. 6 years old
    B. 7 years old
    C. 8 years old
    D. 9 years old

26. Which of the following are primary issuers of individual bonds?

    (1) Local government
    (2) US government
    (3) An agency of the US government
    (4) Corporations

    A. (1) and (4) only
    B. (1), (2), and (3) only
    C. (2), (3), and (4) only
    D. All of the above

27. **Which of the following are tax-free fringe benefits a doctor may provide to her employees?**

    (1) Group disability benefits up to 50% of salary
    (2) 30% off medical procedures
    (3) $50 per month for parking
    (4) Occasional theatre tickets

    A. (1) and (2) only
    B. (3) and (4) only
    C. (1), (3), and (4) only
    D. All of the above

28. **A plan is considered to be informally funded if which of the following conditions apply?**

    (1) The employee has no rights or secured interest in the benefit.
    (2) The benefit is always subject to the claims of the company's creditors.
    (3) The benefit consists of life insurance, mutual funds, or other securities.
    (4) A promise to pay is the employee's only security of future benefits.

    A. (1) and (2) only
    B. (1), (3), and (4) only
    C. (2), (3), and (4) only
    D. All of the above

29. **Which of the following investment strategies will expose an investor to the greatest amount of risk?**

    A. Selling a covered call
    B. Selling a naked call
    C. Buying a naked call
    D. Buying a covered call

30. Which of the following describes the failure of a gift of property to be distributed according to the provisions of a will because the property no longer belongs to the testator at the time of death?

   A. Rescission
   B. Abatement
   C. Reformation
   D. Ademption

31. Which of the following are correct regarding the exclusion of EE bond interest from a taxpayer's gross income?

   (1) The bond must have been issued after December 31, 1994.
   (2) The exclusion is phased out for higher income taxpayers.
   (3) The bond must have been issued to an individual who was at least 21 years old at the time of issuance.
   (4) The exclusion is not available for married taxpayers filing separately.

   A. (1) and (3) only
   B. (2) and (4) only
   C. (1), (2), and (4) only
   D. All of the above

32. Noah wants to receive the equivalent of $60,000 in today's dollars at the beginning of each year for the next 25 years. He assumes inflation will average 8%, and that he can earn a 6% compound annual rate of return on his investments. How much does Noah need to invest today in order to achieve his goal?

   A. $1,187,125.89
   B. $1,209,524.50
   C. $1,894,279.39
   D. $1,930,033.73

33. Which of the following is/are correct regarding closed-end mutual funds?

   (1) Closed-end mutual funds may issue new shares when an individual buys existing shares.
   (2) Closed-end mutual funds may sell at a premium or discount to their net asset value.

   A. (1) only
   B. (2) only
   C. None of the above
   D. All of the above

34. Michelle owns a house she would like to pass to her nephew at death. Rather than wait, she gives the house to her nephew today with the stipulation that she will continue to live in the house for the rest of her life. Which of the following interests has Michelle given to her nephew?

   A. A life estate interest
   B. A remainder interest
   C. A reversionary interest
   D. A term interest

35. Which of the following is/are correct regarding liquidity and marketability?

   (1) Liquidity is the ability to sell or redeem an investment quickly and at a known price without incurring a significant loss of principal.
   (2) Marketability is the speed and ease with which a security may be bought or sold.

   A. (1) only
   B. (2) only
   C. None of the above
   D. All of the above

36. According to Principle of _____, a **CFP**® Board designee shall return a client's original records in a timely manner after their return has been requested by the client.

A. Professionalism
B. Integrity
C. Confidentiality
D. Fairness

37. Which of the following types of property are eligible for a like-kind exchange?

(1) Common stock
(2) Inventory
(3) Rental property
(4) Raw material

A. (3) only
B. (3) and (4) only
C. (1), (2), and (4) only
D. (2), (3), and (4) only

38. Mike purchased a boat for $10,500. He is financing the boat at 11% compounded monthly for 4 years. How much is Mike required to pay at the end of each month to finance the boat?

A. $264.25
B. $266.47
C. $268.91
D. $271.38

39. Which of the following will decrease an employer's contribution to a defined benefit plan?

(1) High ratio of married to unmarried participants
(2) Large forfeitures
(3) Lower than expected investment returns
(4) High turnover among employees

A. (1) and (2) only
B. (1) and (3) only
C. (2) and (3) only
D. (2) and (4) only

40. All but which of the following are correct regarding the lifetime learning credit?

A. It is a nonrefundable credit of up to $2,000.
B. The credit is equal to 20% of qualified education expenses up to $10,000.
C. The credit is available annually for an unlimited number of years.
D. The credit is available for undergraduate students only.

For questions 41-45, match the investment with the description that follows. Use only one answer per blank. Each answer may be used only once.

A. Money market fund
B. Corporate bond
C. Common stock
D. Mutual fund
E. Real estate

41. _____ Diversification smoothes price volatility, historical above-inflation return, can preserve purchasing power in a portfolio

42. _____ Liquid, easily converted to cash, low default risk, low real return

43. _____ Fixed return, may lose value if not held until maturity, fixed interest payments

44. _____ Not liquid, generally adequate inflation hedge

45. _____ Used to generate income and growth, marketable, historical above-inflation return, can preserve purchasing power in a portfolio

46. Chapter 7 bankruptcy involves _____ of assets. Chapter 13 bankruptcy involves _____ of debt.

    A. reorganization, liquidation
    B. reorganization, reorganization
    C. liquidation, reorganization
    D. liquidation, liquidation

47. Which of the following are permitted investments in a 403b plan?

    (1) Mutual funds
    (2) Individual bonds
    (3) Treasury bills
    (4) Life insurance if it is incidental to an annuity contract

    A. (2) and (3) only
    B. (1) and (4) only
    C. (1), (2), and (3) only
    D. All of the above

48. Which of the following will result if an insured of a life insurance policy dies during the grace period and the premium has not yet been paid?

    A. The prorated premium will be subtracted from the death benefit and the remainder will be paid to the beneficiary.
    B. It will be assumed the premium was paid and there will be no reduction in death benefit.
    C. The policy will lapse and no death benefit will be paid.
    D. None of the above are correct.

49. Which of the following is/are correct regarding net operating losses (NOLs)?

    (1) Net operating losses have a two-year carry back period.
    (2) Net operating losses have a ten-year carry forward period.

    A. (1) only
    B. (2) only
    C. None of the above
    D. All of the above

For questions 50-54, match the source of tax authority with the description that follows. Use only one answer per blank. Answers may be used more than once or not at all.

A. Treasury Regulations
B. Revenue Rulings
C. Private Letter Rulings
D. Revenue Procedures
E. Technical Advice Memorandum

50. _____ Generally related to compliance matters such as tax tables, inflation indexed amounts, and asset class lives. They deal with the technical rather than substantive matters of tax law.

51. _____ Direct extension of the law-making powers of Congress. Next to the Internal Revenue Code, these are the highest source of authority.

52. _____ Guidance provided by the Office of Chief Counsel upon the request of an IRS director in response to technical questions that develop during a proceeding.

53. _____ Provide interpretations of tax law and give guidance to taxpayers. They are generally binding on all taxpayers.

54. _____ Specific interpretations related to the tax consequences of a transaction at the request of a taxpayer. They are only binding on the taxpayer that requests the ruling.

55. Timmy, age 13, works for his father developing children's computer games. His father owns and operates a sole proprietorship. Timmy is paid $15,000 annually for his work. What is Timmy's tax bracket for the majority of his earnings?

A. His father's tax bracket with a reduction for social security
B. His father's tax bracket without a reduction for social security
C. Timmy's tax bracket with a reduction for social security
D. Timmy's tax bracket without a reduction for social security

56. A benefit plan is considered to be _____ if assets are set aside in a general reserve fund to meet the benefit obligations of the plan.

A. funded
B. informally funded
C. conditionally funded
D. unfunded

57. Which of the following describes how much a donor is permitted to deduct for a contribution of his or her time or services to a qualified charity?

A. 20% of AGI
B. 30% of AGI
C. 50% of AGI
D. No deduction is allowed.

58. Which of the following is not a basic form of covered peril found in homeowners insurance policies?

A. Hail
B. Riot
C. Falling objects
D. Windstorm

59. If a married couple rents out their beach house for five months of the year, how many days can they personally use the house without losing federal income tax deductions?

A. 0 days
B. 7 days
C. 14 days
D. 15 days

For questions 60-66, match the type of retirement plan with the description that follows. Use only one answer per blank. Answers may be used more than once or not at all.

    A. Profit sharing plan
    B. Pension plan

60. ____ 401k plan

61. ____ Money purchase plan

62. ____ Stock bonus plan

63. ____ ESOP

64. ____ Target benefit plan

65. ____ Thrift savings plan

66. ____ Cash balance plan

67. If a terminated employee converts a group term life insurance policy to an individual cash value policy, how is the new premium calculated?

    A. The premium is based on the employee's age on the date the group term policy was issued.
    B. The premium is based on the employee's health on the date the group term policy was issued.
    C. The premium is based on the employee's age on the conversion date.
    D. The premium is based on the employee's health on the conversion date.

68. In order for group term life insurance to be excluded from an employee's income it must satisfy which of the following requirements?

(1) Must provide a general death benefit which is includible in income
(2) Must be provided to a group of employees
(3) Must be provided under a policy carried directly or indirectly by the employer
(4) Amount of insurance provided to each employee cannot be based on age, years of service, compensation, or position

A. (1) and (4) only
B. (2) and (3) only
C. (1), (2), and (3) only
D. (2), (3), and (4) only

69. Which of the following are correct regarding universal life policies with the "Option B" death benefit?

(1) The death benefit includes the cash accumulation fund.
(2) The death benefit is equal to the face amount of the policy plus the accumulation fund.
(3) The mortality charges are based on the net amount at risk, which is the face amount of the policy minus the accumulation fund.
(4) The mortality charges are based on the face amount of the policy every year.

A. (1) and (3) only
B. (1) and (4) only
C. (2) and (3) only
D. (2) and (4) only

70. The first required minimum distribution from a traditional IRA must be taken by _____ of the year following the calendar year in which the participant turns age _____.

A. April 1, 71
B. December 31, 70 ½
C. April 1, 70 ½
D. December 31, 70

71. **How is the adjusted basis of an asset calculated? Assume the asset was originally acquired at an arm's length transaction from a non-related party.**

    A. Cost minus expenses of sale plus depreciation and amortization
    B. Cost plus expenses of sale plus depreciation and amortization
    C. Cost plus expenses of sale less depreciation and amortization
    D. Cost minus expenses of sale less depreciation and amortization

72. **All but which of the following are exempt from COBRA coverage?**

    A. Government employers
    B. Employers with less than 30 employees
    C. Church employers
    D. All of the above are exempt from COBRA coverage.

For questions 73-76, match the depreciation time period with the description that follows. Use only one answer per blank. Answers may be used more than once or not at all.

    A. 5 years
    B. 7 years
    C. 27.5 years
    D. 39 years

73. _____ **Useful life of residential rental property**

74. _____ **Useful life of office equipment except computers**

75. _____ **Useful life of autos, light-duty trucks, and computers**

76. _____ **Useful life of commercial rental property**

77. **For a qualified retirement plan to pass the percentage test, the plan must benefit at least _____ of all employees who are not highly compensated.**

    A. 50%
    B. 60%
    C. 70%
    D. 75%

78. If a company has three owners, how many life insurance policies will be purchased if a cross-purchase agreement is used?

    A. 3
    B. 6
    C. 9
    D. 12

79. Employees pay a social security payroll tax of _____ on all wages up to the social security wage base. An additional tax of _____ is paid by each employee to fund Medicare, for a combined payroll tax of _____ for each employee.

    A. 1.45%, 6.2%, 7.65%
    B. 6.2%, 1.45%, 7.65%
    C. 6.25%, 1.5%, 7.75%
    D. 1.5%, 6.25%, 7.75%

80. Which of the following describes a type of split-dollar life insurance coverage in which the insured pays the portion of the premium that supports the death benefit, and when the insured dies the other party recovers its investment and the beneficiary receives the death benefit, less any amount owed to the other party, tax free?

    A. Endorsement method
    B. Entity purchase method
    C. Key employee method
    D. Collateral assignment method

81. An individual who gifts his or her assets to another person or entity within _____ of applying for Medicaid will be subject to an enrollment penalty.

    A. 1 year
    B. 2 years
    C. 5 years
    D. 7 years

For questions 82-85, determine if the exchange described qualifies as a 1035 exchange. Use only one answer per blank. Answers may be used more than once or not at all.

    A. 1035 exchange
    B. Not a 1035 exchange

82. _____ **A life insurance policy exchanged for a life insurance policy**

83. _____ **An annuity exchanged for an annuity**

84. _____ **An annuity exchanged for a life insurance policy**

85. _____ **A life insurance policy exchanged for an annuity**

86. **An HO-4 insurance policy has which of the following characteristics?**

    A. Provides all-risk coverage on other structures
    B. Excludes coverage for personal liability
    C. Provides all-risk coverage on personal property
    D. Provides no coverage on the dwelling

87. **To qualify for the Section 2032A "special use valuation", qualifying real property must have been owned by the decedent or a member of his or her family for a period of at least _____ out of the prior _____ ending on the date of the decedent's death.**

    A. 3 years, 5 years
    B. 4 years, 6 years
    C. 5 years, 8 years
    D. 6 years, 10 years

88. **A variable life insurance policy has which of the following characteristics?**

    A. A minimum death benefit is guaranteed.
    B. Premiums and death benefits are flexible.
    C. It is made up of increasing units of term insurance and a guaranteed cash value.
    D. The death benefit is linked to the performance of the Dow Jones stock average only.

89. An S Corp holds which of the following advantages over a personal service corporation (PSC)?

A. S Corps provide limited liability; PSCs do not.
B. S Corps provide a step-up in basis at death; PSCs do not.
C. S Corps pass through earnings and losses; PSCs do not.
D. S Corps allow deductions for business expenses; PSCs do not.

90. The category or risk in which loss is the only possible outcome is known as _____.

A. gambling
B. pure risk
C. speculative risk
D. investment risk

91. Travis creates an irrevocable trust to which he contributes income producing property. The trust will pay Travis income for life equal to 6% of the value of the trust revalued annually. At the death of Travis, the trust corpus will be paid to the Red Cross. Which type of trust did Travis create?

A. Charitable remainder annuity trust (CRAT)
B. Charitable remainder unitrust (CRUT)
C. Charitable lead unitrust (CLUT)
D. Charitable lead annuity trust (CLAT)

92. The part of Medicare that pays for hospital expenses, but not physician's charges is _____.

A. Medicare Part A
B. Medicare Part B
C. Medicare Part C
D. Medicare Part D

93. Which of the following is a characteristic of participating life insurance policies?

A. Only mutual insurance companies can issue policies that pay dividends.
B. Insurers are allowed to guarantee future dividends for a maximum of one year.
C. Policy dividends are partly a return of a deliberate overcharge of premium by the insurer.
D. Any dividends paid are fully tax deductible.

94. If property that could otherwise be valued with use of the alternate valuation date is sold prior to the six-month valuation date, how is the value of the property determined for estate tax purposes?

A. The property is valued at its sale price unless it is greater than the date of death value.
B. The property is valued at its date of death value.
C. The property is valued at its sale price.
D. None of the above are correct.

95. Decreasing term life insurance is characterized by a _____ premium and _____ face amount of coverage.

A. decreasing, increasing
B. decreasing, decreasing
C. level, decreasing
D. decreasing, level

96. The annual payout rate for a CRUT must be at least _____ of the current fair market value of trust assets.

A. 1%
B. 5%
C. 6%
D. 10%

97. If a qualified disclaimer is made, the beneficiary that disclaims is considered to have _____ the property and _____ a subsequent gift.

    A. received, received
    B. received, made
    C. never received, has not made
    D. None of the above are correct.

98. The three categories of hazards are _____, _____, and _____.

    A. perils, hazards, risks
    B. moral, morale, physical
    C. life, disability, long-term care
    D. property, casualty, physical

99. To be legally effective, all trusts must have which of the following?

    (1) Grantor
    (2) Trustee
    (3) Trust corpus
    (4) Beneficiary

    A. (1) and (2) only
    B. (1) and (3) only
    C. (1), (2), and (4) only
    D. None of the above

100. Which of the following are correct regarding Roth IRAs?

    (1) Contributions to a Roth IRA can be made at any age.
    (2) Contributions to a Roth IRA must be made before age 70 ½.
    (3) A Roth IRA owner is not required to take a minimum distribution during his or her lifetime.
    (4) Roth IRA contributions may be deducted in limited circumstances.

    A. (1) and (3) only
    B. (2) and (3) only
    C. (1), (3), and (4) only
    D. (2), (3), and (4) only

101. **For a reverse gift, a step-up in basis is not allowed if the donee/decedent dies within _____ of receiving a gift and then transfers the property back to the original donor.**

    A. 6 months
    B. 9 months
    C. 1 year
    D. 2 years

102. **The EAFE Index is a _____ weighted index of the _____ performance of major foreign markets.**

    A. value, fixed-income
    B. price, equity
    C. value, equity
    D. price, fixed-income

103. **A QDOT is not necessary if a _____ spouse dies first and leaves all of his or her property to a _____ spouse.**

    A. US citizen, non-citizen
    B. non-citizen, US citizen
    C. None of the above are correct.
    D. All of the above are correct.

104. **Which of the following are backed by the full faith and credit of the government issuing the bonds and are repaid through taxes collected by the government body?**

    A. Revenue bonds
    B. Government bonds
    C. General obligation bonds
    D. Private purpose bonds

105. Which of the following is/are correct regarding a QPRT?

(1) A QPRT is generally appropriate for vacation homes valued at over $1 million.
(2) A QPRT is ideal for a single parent in his or her 30s or 40s.
(3) The grantor will have a taxable gift upon the creation of a QPRT.
(4) After the trust term ends, the house reverts back to the grantor.

A. (1) only
B. (1) and (3) only
C. (2) and (4) only
D. (1), (3), and (4) only

106. The efficient market hypothesis suggests all but which of the following?

A. Investors are unable to outperform the stock market on a consistent basis.
B. Any excess returns are temporary and will regress to the mean.
C. The stock market's efficiency in valuing securities is rapid and accurate.
D. Daily fluctuations in stock prices are a result of Modern Portfolio Theory.

107. Incentive stock options (ISOs) may be granted to which of the following?

A. Non-employee directors
B. Employees
C. Independent contractors
D. All of the above are correct.

108. A living will has which of the following characteristics?

(1) Has the same function as a revocable living trust
(2) Allows an individual to appoint property before death
(3) Allows an individual to specify wishes about medical treatment and artificial life support under specific circumstances
(4) May be referred to as an advance medical directive

A. (1) and (2) only
B. (3) and (4) only
C. (1), (3), and (4) only
D. All of the above

109. Which of the following is/are correct regarding profit sharing plans?

   (1) Profit sharing plans are a type of defined contribution pension plan.
   (2) The minimum funding standard requires the employer to make an annual contribution.

   A. (1) only
   B. (2) only
   C. None of the above
   D. All of the above

110. Evidence provided of premium payment that accompanies an application for insurance is known as which of the following?

   A. Proof of consideration
   B. Conditional receipt
   C. Conditional contract
   D. Signed receipt

111. Which of the following are among the exemptions from the 10% early withdrawal penalty from an IRA?

   (1) Hardship withdrawals
   (2) Higher education expenses for a participant's child
   (3) First-time home purchase up to $10,000
   (4) Loan for qualified education expenses

   A. (1) and (4) only
   B. (2) and (3) only
   C. (1), (2), and (3) only
   D. All of the above

112. Which of the following requirements must be met in order for a donor to make an inter-vivos gift?

    (1) The donor must be legally competent.
    (2) The donee must be capable of receiving and possessing the property.
    (3) There must be delivery to, and acceptance by, the donee or the donee's agent.
    (4) The donor must make a "complete" gift.

    A. (1) and (3) only
    B. (2) and (4) only
    C. (1), (2), and (3) only
    D. All of the above

113. In a defined contribution plan, the premiums paid for whole life insurance coverage cannot exceed _____ of the contributions made to the plan on the participant's behalf.

    A. 10%
    B. 25%
    C. 50%
    D. 100%

114. Which of the following describes the taxation of an annuity owned by a decedent?

    A. The decedent's will determines who will receive the proceeds of an annuity.
    B. Accumulated interest is income tax free.
    C. Unpaid interest is considered income in respect of a decedent (IRD).
    D. None of the above are correct.

115. An employee is an active participant in a defined benefit plan if he or she meets which of the following requirements?

(1) The employee actively participates in the plan.
(2) The employee meets the eligibility requirements at any time during the plan year.
(3) The employee is eligible to participate in the plan but declines to participate.
(4) The employee receives plan forfeitures only.

A. (1) and (4) only
B. (2) and (3) only
C. (2), (3), and (4) only
D. All of the above

116. Which of the following is/are correct regarding gift splitting?

(1) Gift splitting may be used on a gift-by-gift basis during a calendar year.
(2) Both spouses must consent to the use of gift splitting. However, if no gift tax is due then a gift tax return is not necessary.

A. (1) only
B. (2) only
C. None of the above
D. All of the above

117. Gifts made during a donor's lifetime receive a _____ of basis, and gifts made at death receive a _____ of basis.

A. carryover, step-up
B. step-up, carryover
C. carryover, carryover
D. step-up, step-up

118. Which of the following theories is based on the assumption that investors are risk-averse, and for a given level of risk investors prefer higher returns to lower returns?

A. Arbitrage Pricing Theory
B. Black-Scholes Valuation Theory
C. Modern Portfolio Theory
D. Efficient Market Theory

119. Which of the following is/are correct regarding loan provisions in a **SIMPLE** plan?

   (1) Loans from a **SIMPLE IRA** are not permitted.
   (2) Loans from a **SIMPLE 401k** are permitted.

   A. (1) only
   B. (2) only
   C. None of the above
   D. All of the above

For questions 120-123, determine how the property listed will pass at the owner's death. Use only one answer per blank. Answers may be used more than once or not at all.

   A. The property will pass by operation of law
   B. The property will pass by contract
   C. The property will pass by trust

120. ____ **401k naming a spouse as beneficiary**

121. ____ **Home titled JTWROS between a brother and sister**

122. ____ **Home titled tenancy by entirety between a husband and wife**

123. ____ **A life insurance policy naming a sibling as beneficiary**

124. Which of the following is/are correct regarding open-end mutual funds?

   (1) Open-end mutual funds sell at their net asset value (NAV).
   (2) Open-end mutual funds have a fixed capital structure.

   A. (1) only
   B. (2) only
   C. None of the above
   D. All of the above

125. The payout rate for a charitable remainder trust must be between _____ at a minimum and _____ at a maximum.

    A. 5%, 25%
    B. 10%, 50%
    C. 10%, 25%
    D. 5%, 50%

126. All but which of the following are characteristics of a REIT?

    A. Losses cannot be passed through to investors to deduct personally.
    B. REIT shareholders are subject to double taxation.
    C. REITs can be purchased in small denominations.
    D. All of the above are characteristics of a REIT.

127. Which of the following accurately describe "defensive stocks"?

    A. Stocks that invest in the defense sector of the US economy.
    B. Stocks that are tax efficient and therefore "defensive" for tax purposes.
    C. Stocks that are unaffected by changes in interest rates.
    D. Stocks that are unaffected by general fluctuations in the economy.

128. Which of the following retirement plans would be most suitable to retain young employees?

    A. Money purchase plan
    B. Defined benefit plan
    C. Target benefit plan
    D. Cash balance plan

129.Which of the following is/are correct regarding lifetime gifts?

(1) A donee's basis is decreased by any gift tax paid.
(2) When a donor's basis exceeds the fair market value of the property, the donee has two bases. One basis is for subsequent gain, and the other is for subsequent loss.

A. (1) only
B. (2) only
C. None of the above
D. All of the above

130.The standard expiration period for a put or call option is _____. Long-term equity anticipation securities (LEAPS) have an expiration period _____.

A. 6 months, longer than 1 year
B. 9 months, between 9 months and 1 year
C. 6 months, between 6 months and 1 year
D. 9 months, longer than 1 year

131.Which of the following is/are correct regarding the objectives of ERISA?

(1) ERISA requires plan sponsors to disclose full and accurate information about qualified retirement plan activity to all participants.
(2) ERISA guarantees future benefits at a minimum level for defined benefit plans as part of the PBGC.

A. (1) only
B. (2) only
C. None of the above
D. All of the above

132.A trust is established and funded with an initial gift of $250,000. Crummey powers are attached to the trust. If the beneficiary chooses to exercise his demand right, how much can he withdraw during the first thirty days?

A. $0
B. $5,000
C. $12,500
D. Up to the gift tax annual exclusion

133. **All but which of the following are correct regarding the correlation coefficient?**

   A. Two securities that have a correlation coefficient of +1 are perfectly positively correlated. The two securities will move in the exact same direction.
   B. Two securities that have a correlation coefficient of -1 are perfectly negatively correlated. The two securities will move exactly opposite each other.
   C. If two securities have a correlation coefficient of zero, there is no correlation between the price changes of the two securities.
   D. Risk is eliminated when the correlation coefficient between two securities is zero because the portfolio standard deviation will also be zero.

134. **For incentive stock options (ISOs), an employee must be employed by the same company without interruption from the time the option is granted until _____ or less before the date of exercise.**

   A. 3 months
   B. 6 months
   C. 1 year
   D. 2 years

135. **Which of the following is/are correct regarding the tax treatment of an installment sale?**

   (1) **If a seller dies during the installment period of an installment sale, the present value of any future payments yet to be received by the seller are excluded from the seller's gross estate.**
   (2) **If a seller survives the installment period of an installment sale, the property sold reverts back to the seller's gross estate.**

   A. (1) only
   B. (2) only
   C. None of the above
   D. All of the above

136. If an investment is held for more than one year, the holding period return _____ the true return on an annual basis. If an investment is held for less than one year, the holding period return _____ the true investment return.

    A. understates, overstates
    B. overstates, understates
    C. overstates, correctly states
    D. correctly states, overstates

137. All but which of the following are characteristics of American Depository Receipts (ADRs)?

    A. ADR dividends are declared in US dollars.
    B. ADRs trade throughout the day like stocks.
    C. ADR holders receive foreign tax credits for income tax paid to a foreign country.
    D. ADRs allow for the trading of international securities in domestic countries.

138. Ben purchased 100 shares of LMN stock for $50 per share. At the end of two years, he sold the shares for $70 per share. In the first year, the stock did not pay a dividend. In the second year, the stock paid a $3 dividend. What was the holding period return of Ben's investment?

    A. 23%
    B. 26%
    C. 32%
    D. 46%

139. For incentive stock options (ISOs), if the fair market value of the stock exceeds $100,000 at the time of grant, which of the following will result?

    A. The amount in excess of $100,000 is treated as an ISO with different tax treatment.
    B. The amount in excess of $100,000 is treated as an NQSO with different tax treatment.
    C. The amount in excess of $100,000 is taxed at capital gains rates.
    D. None of the above are correct.

140. In which of the following circumstances will a standard power of attorney lapse?

   A. When the principal dies
   B. When the agent dies
   C. When the principal becomes mentally incapacitated
   D. All of the above are correct.

141. Which of the following is/are correct regarding dividends paid by growth stocks and value stocks?

   (1) Because they are growing and expanding, growth stocks typically do not pay large dividends.
   (2) Most of the earnings generated from value stocks are reinvested back into the company.

   A. (1) only
   B. (2) only
   C. None of the above
   D. All of the above

142. Which of the following are permitted investments in an IRA?

   (1) Real estate
   (2) Money market funds
   (3) Common stock
   (4) Bond funds

   A. (3) and (4) only
   B. (1), (2), and (3) only
   C. (2), (3), and (4) only
   D. All of the above

143. Tyler inherited shares of **ABC** stock that are currently valued at $500,000. In order to retire comfortably, Tyler requires a fixed 7% payout for life. Which of the following trusts will allow Tyler to achieve his goal?

A. CRUT
B. CLAT
C. CRAT
D. CLUT

144. Book value is calculated through which of the following methods?

A. Book value = total assets − (intangible assets + liabilities)
B. Book value = tangible assets + intangible assets - liabilities
C. Book value = total assets − (intangible assets - liabilities)
D. Book value = tangible assets − intangible assets + liabilities

145. Which of the following is/are correct regarding death benefit only (DBO) plans?

(1) DBO plans must be funded through life insurance only.
(2) A DBO plan is a type of deferred compensation plan under which all benefits are payable upon death to the beneficiaries designated by the employee.

A. (1) only
B. (2) only
C. None of the above
D. All of the above

146. According to the anomaly known as the P/E effect, _____ P/E stocks appear to outperform _____ P/E stocks over annual periods after being adjusted for risk and size.

A. high, low
B. low, high
C. average, low
D. high, average

147. **In order to qualify for social security disability benefits, a worker must meet which of the following definitions of disability?**

A. Unable to perform the duties of his or her own occupation
B. Unable to perform any substantial gainful activity
C. Unable to perform the duties of his or her own occupation for one year, then unable to perform any substantial gainful activity thereafter
D. Unable to perform the duties of his or her own occupation for two years, then unable to perform any substantial gainful activity thereafter

148. **If a wash sale occurs, which of the following will result?**

A. No loss deduction is allowed, and the amount of the disallowed loss is subtracted from the cost basis of the newly acquired shares.
B. The loss can be realized.
C. No loss deduction is allowed, and a gain must be realized immediately.
D. No loss deduction is allowed, and the amount of the disallowed loss is added to the cost basis of the newly acquired shares.

149. **Under the social security system, a fully insured worker is one that has paid into the system for at least _____ during his or her employment career.**

A. 10 quarters
B. 20 quarters
C. 32 quarters
D. 40 quarters

150. **Assume that Portfolio X has a return of 15%, a standard deviation of 7%, and a beta of 2.0. The risk-free rate of return is 4%. What is the Sharpe ratio for Portfolio X?**

A. 0.06
B. 1.57
C. 1.85
D. 2.14

151. A group term life insurance policy can be converted to an individual life policy within _____ of an employee terminating employment.

    A. 14 days
    B. 31 days
    C. 61 days
    D. 90 days

152. Which of the following theories states that security prices in different markets will not differ for any significant period of time?

    A. Arbitrage Pricing Theory
    B. Black-Scholes Valuation Theory
    C. Efficient Market Theory
    D. Modern Portfolio Theory

153. For an employee that is covered by her large employer's health insurance plan, how long must she work to ensure she maintains health coverage? Assume the employee will not qualify for health insurance through a private insurer.

    A. Until age 61 ½
    B. Until age 63 ½
    C. Until age 65
    D. The employee can retire today.

154. The S&P index has _____ risk.

    A. unsystematic
    B. non-systematic
    C. non-diversifiable
    D. diversifiable

155. Which of the following is/are correct regarding use of the marital deduction?

    (1) There may be a requirement that the surviving spouse survive the decedent by a period not to exceed six months.
    (2) If the decedent was not a US citizen, a QDOT is required in order to qualify property for the marital deduction.

    A. (1) only
    B. (2) only
    C. None of the above
    D. All of the above

156. Security A has an expected return of 9% and a standard deviation of 10%. Security B has an expected return of 5% and a standard deviation of 8%. Which security is more suitable for a risk-averse investor?

    A. Security A because it has a lower coefficient of variation
    B. Security A because it has a higher coefficient of variation
    C. Security B because it has a lower coefficient of variation
    D. Security B because it has a higher coefficient of variation

157. If a spouse waives her right to a pre-retirement survivor annuity and a joint and survivor annuity, which of the following is correct?

    A. The waiver is revocable.
    B. The spouse is not required to sign a written waiver.
    C. If a waiver is signed, it must be witnessed by a notary or by an official of the plan.
    D. None of the above are correct.

158. Assume that stock A has a standard deviation of 6.5% and stock B has a standard deviation of 12.4%. The correlation coefficient between the two stocks is +0.30. What is the covariance of the two stocks?

    A. 22.46
    B. 23.38
    C. 24.18
    D. 25.26

159. Health insurance premiums paid by an employer are excluded from an employee's income if which of the following individuals are covered?

   (1) The employee's spouse
   (2) The employee's dependent child
   (3) The employee, if retired
   (4) The employee, if currently employed

   A. (3) and (4) only
   B. (1), (2), and (3) only
   C. (1), (2), and (4) only
   D. All of the above

160. Which of the following is/are correct regarding a bond's interest rate and term to maturity?

   (1) The lower a bond's interest rate, the lower its relative price fluctuation.
   (2) The longer a bond's term to maturity, the greater its relative price fluctuation.

   A. (1) only
   B. (2) only
   C. None of the above
   D. All of the above

161. Which of the following describes the difference between a 401k plan and a 403b plan?

   A. A 401k plan is a qualified plan, but a 403b plan is not a qualified plan.
   B. A 403b plan is a qualified plan, but a 401k plan is not a qualified plan.
   C. A 401k plan allows loans, but a 403b plan does not allow loans.
   D. A 501(c)(3) organization may establish a 403b plan but cannot establish a 401k plan.

For questions 162-164, match the real estate investment with the description that follows. Use only one answer per blank. Answers may be used more than once or not at all.

A. Equity REIT
B. Mortgage REIT
C. Real Estate Mortgage Investment Conduit (REMIC)

162. ____ Invests in loans secured by real estate

163. ____ Self-liquidating, flow-through entity that invests in real estate mortgages or mortgage-backed securities

164. ____ Acquires ownership interests in commercial, industrial, and residential properties. Income is received from the rental of these properties.

165. Mark, an elderly business owner, is interested in establishing a retirement plan that will provide the greatest retirement benefit to himself. Which of the following plans should Mark select?

A. Defined contribution plan
B. Defined benefit plan
C. Money purchase plan
D. 401k plan

166. Which of the following types of coverage may be provided by long-term care policies?

(1) Skilled nursing care
(2) Intermediate nursing care
(3) Home health care
(4) Custodial care

A. (1) and (4) only
B. (3) and (4) only
C. (1), (2), and (3) only
D. All of the above

167. Which of the following plans require immediate vesting?

(1) **Money purchase plan**
(2) **SEP**
(3) **403b plan**
(4) **SARSEP**

A. (2) only
B. (1) and (3) only
C. (2) and (4) only
D. All of the above

168. Which of the following investment strategies are profitable in a rising stock market?

(1) **Buying a call**
(2) **Buying a put**
(3) **Selling a put**
(4) **Selling a call**

A. (1) and (3) only
B. (1) and (4) only
C. (2) and (3) only
D. (2) and (4) only

169. A special catch up provision is permitted in 403b plans for employees with at least _____ of service who have not made contributions and are employed by universities.

A. 5 years
B. 10 years
C. 15 years
D. 20 years

170. A _____ provides the decedent/grantor's estate with the unlimited marital deduction while, at the same time, ensuring the decedent retains control over the ultimate disposition of his or her property.

    A. marital trust
    B. credit shelter trust
    C. QTIP trust
    D. revocable trust

171. A loss on the sale of securities is not deductible if a taxpayer purchases identical securities within _____ prior to or after the date of sale.

    A. 7 days
    B. 14 days
    C. 30 days
    D. 60 days

For questions 172-175, match the retirement plan with the description that follows. Use only one answer per blank. Each answer may be used only once.

    A. Profit sharing plan
    B. Money purchase plan
    C. Cash balance plan
    D. Target benefit plan

172. _____ A plan that requires a fixed percentage of compensation to be contributed for each eligible employee.

173. _____ A plan similar to a defined benefit plan because contributions are based on projected retirement benefits.

174. _____ A type of defined contribution plan that is not a pension plan.

175. _____ A defined benefit plan that defines an employee's benefit in terms that are more characteristic with a defined contribution plan.

176. According to the Principle of _____, a **CFP®** Board designee shall exercise reasonable and prudent professional judgment in providing professional services to clients.

    A. Professionalism
    B. Diligence
    C. Objectivity
    D. Fairness

177. All but which of the following are characteristics of a defined benefit plan?

    A. Actuarial calculations are required
    B. Employee assumes the investment risk
    C. Favors older employees
    D. None of the above are correct.

178. By adding a _____ provision to a trust, a grantor is allowing for certain future financial circumstances among beneficiaries that he or she cannot foresee at the present time.

    A. reallocation
    B. reversion
    C. rescission
    D. sprinkling

179. Legal expenses incurred by a taxpayer in connection with being represented in a tax audit are _____. Legal expenses incurred by a taxpayer in connection with defending title to a property are _____.

    A. non-deductible, non-deductible
    B. deductible, deductible
    C. non-deductible, deductible
    D. deductible, non-deductible

180. A QDOT must meet all but which of the following requirements if property passing to a surviving spouse is to qualify for the marital deduction?

A. The trust must require at least one trustee to be a US citizen or US corporation.

B. The non-citizen surviving spouse must receive at least 50% of the income from the trust.

C. The trustee of the QDOT must have the right to withhold federal estate tax on distributions of principal to the non-citizen surviving spouse.

D. The executor of the decedent's estate must make an election on IRS Form 706 to qualify property for the marital deduction.

181. COBRA continuation coverage is provided to which of the following employees?

(1) Employees who are voluntarily terminated for gross misconduct

(2) Employees who are voluntarily terminated for reasons except gross misconduct

(3) Employees who are involuntarily terminated for gross misconduct

(4) Employees who are involuntarily terminated for reasons except gross misconduct

A. (2) only

B. (2) and (4) only

C. (1), (2), and (4) only

D. All of the above

182. Interest earned on _____ is a tax preference item for AMT.

A. revenue bonds

B. general obligation bonds

C. public purpose bonds

D. private activity bonds

183. All but which of the following are correct regarding the Section 121 exclusion?

A. Section 121 permits an exclusion of up to $250,000 of taxable gain on the sale of a principal residence for a single taxpayer.

B. The owner must satisfy the "distance" test in order to use the Section 121 exclusion.

C. The owner must satisfy the "use" test in order to use the Section 121 exclusion.

D. Section 121 permits an exclusion of up to $500,000 of taxable gain on the sale of a principal residence for married couples filing a joint tax return.

184. Meals are excluded from an employee's gross income if they are:

A. provided by the employer.
B. provided on the employer's premises.
C. provided for the convenience of the employee.
D. Both A and B are correct.

185. Which of the following describe the maturities of Treasury bills, Treasury notes, and Treasury bonds?

A. Treasury notes have maturities of 10 years or more.
B. Treasury bills have maturities of 1 year or more.
C. Treasury bonds have maturities greater than 10 years.
D. All of the above are correct.

186. The gift tax annual exclusion is permitted for:

A. present interest gifts only.
B. future interest gifts only.
C. present and future interest gifts.
D. any completed gift that does not revert back to the grantor.

187. Viatical payments to a terminally ill insured are _____ if he or she has a life expectancy of _____.

A. taxable, two years or less
B. non-taxable, two years or less
C. taxable, three years or less
D. non-taxable, two years or more

188. Which of the following is/are correct regarding secular trusts?

    (1) A secular trust is an irrevocable trust set up by an employer to provide nonqualified benefits to an employee.
    (2) Employer contributions to a secular trust are subject to the claims of the company's creditors.

    A. (1) only
    B. (2) only
    C. None of the above
    D. All of the above

189. Which of the following groups may be eligible to participate in a 403b plan?

    A. Public school employees
    B. Not-for-profit hospital employees
    C. Church employees
    D. All of the above are correct.

190. In a long call, the maximum gain is _____ and the maximum loss is _____.

    A. unlimited, the premium
    B. the premium, unlimited
    C. limited, unlimited
    D. unlimited, unlimited

191. An individual can avoid paying the excise tax for over contributing to an IRA if he or she withdrawals the excess contribution and earnings:

    A. before the due date of the federal income tax return.
    B. by December 31 of the year the contribution was made.
    C. by December 31 of the year following the year the contribution was made.
    D. by March 15 of the year following the year the contribution was made.

192. Which of the following are correct regarding the role of a trustee?

   (1) A trustee is the legal owner of trust property.
   (2) A trustee has a fiduciary duty to income beneficiaries only.
   (3) A trustee must act at all times for the exclusive benefit of beneficiaries or he or she may incur a legal liability.
   (4) A trustee has a fiduciary duty to remainder beneficiaries only.

   A. (1) and (3) only
   B. (2) and (4) only
   C. (1), (2), and (3) only
   D. (1), (3), and (4) only

193. Which of the following is correct regarding a bond's coupon rate?

   A. A bond's coupon rate is also its yield to maturity (YTM).
   B. It is the stated annual interest rate that will be paid each period for the term of a bond.
   C. It is stated as a percentage of the current market price of a bond.
   D. A 5% coupon bond will pay $50 each semiannual period for a $1,000 bond.

194. An IRA must be created and funded by _____ of the calendar year following the year in which the contribution applies.

   A. January 1
   B. April 15
   C. June 31
   D. December 31

195. All but which of the following are correct regarding the tenancy by entirety form of property ownership?

   A. It is an interest in property that can be held only by spouses.
   B. The property automatically passes to the surviving spouse when one spouse dies.
   C. In most states, it is not severable by an individual spouse.
   D. It is an interest in property that can be held by non-spouses in an incorporated business such as an LLC, S Corp, or C Corp.

196. Which of the following is not a basic form of covered peril found in homeowners insurance policies?

    A. Smoke
    B. Freezing pipes
    C. Vandalism
    D. Volcanic eruption

197. Which of the following is/are correct regarding stock splits and reverse stock splits?

    (1) A 3-for-1 stock split will decrease a stock's market price per share.
    (2) A reverse stock split is intended to increase a stock's market price per share.

    A. (1) only
    B. (2) only
    C. None of the above
    D. All of the above

198. All but which of the following are characteristics of American Depository Receipts (ADRs)?

    A. Traded on secondary exchanges
    B. Represent ownership interest in foreign securities denominated in US dollars
    C. Banks collect money in US dollars and then convert into foreign currency for ADR holders
    D. Issued by banks in foreign countries

199. Which of the following is/are correct regarding rabbi trusts?

    (1) A rabbi trust may become irrevocable if there is a change in corporate control.
    (2) A rabbi trust creates security for employees because the assets in the trust are outside the employer's control.

    A. (1) only
    B. (2) only
    C. None of the above
    D. All of the above

200.Which of the following techniques can be used to reduce an individual's gross estate, and therefore, reduce estate taxes?

A. Family limited partnership
B. Totten trust
C. POD account
D. Living trust

ANSWER KEY

1. B

According to the Principle of Fairness, a CFP® Board designee's compensation shall be fair and reasonable.

2. C

Alpha = 0.16 − [0.06 + (0.18 - 0.06) × 0.75]
Alpha = 0.16 − [0.06 + 0.09]
Alpha = 0.16 − 0.15
Alpha = 0.01

3. B

Step 1: ($8 × 4) + ($10 × 2) = $52
Step 2: $52 / 6 = $8.67

4. D

Kurtosis measures the thickness of the tail on a normal distribution chart of investment returns.

5. B

According to the common disaster clause, the primary beneficiary of a life insurance policy must survive the insured by a certain number of days in order to receive insurance proceeds. Otherwise the proceeds will be paid to the insured's contingent beneficiary.

6. A

Commercial paper has a maturity of 270 days or less and is issued in denominations of $100,000 or more.

7. D

All of the items listed are required for a buy-sell agreement to be effective.

8. C

Kurtosis measures the thickness of the tail on a normal distribution chart of investment returns. A thin tail (low kurtosis) means investments returns are bunched towards the mean. A risk-averse investor prefers low kurtosis.

9. B
A rabbi trust cannot contain an insolvency trigger. Therefore it cannot be used to protect executives in the event of employer bankruptcy. A rabbi trust can protect executives in the event of a hostile takeover or merger.

10. B
FV = -$15,000
n = 3
i = 8
PV = 0
PMT = ? = $4,620.50

11. B
A skip person for GSTT purposes is a related individual two or more generations below that of the transferor.

12. B
According to the misstatement of age clause, if it is discovered that an insured is older or younger than the age stated on his or her application, the death benefit will be adjusted to what the premiums paid would have purchased if based on the correct age.

13. A
The power to appoint assets to oneself that can be exercised only with the consent of an adverse third-party is a special power of appointment.

14. C
Preferred stock is considered a hybrid security because it has characteristics of both common stock and fixed-income investments.

15. B
Alimony payments are deductible by the payor and taxable to the recipient.

16. A
For married couples, each spouse is entitled to receive a social security benefit based on the greater of his or her own retirement benefit, or 50% of the spouse's benefit.

17. D
The death benefits of a MEC are treated the same as any non-MEC life insurance policy.

18. D
Higher inflation = higher interest rates = lower bond values

19. C

In order for an individual to qualify for Medicaid, he or she must meet both the income test and the asset test.

20. D

An automatic premium loan provision may prevent a life insurance policy from lapsing.

21. D

The SIPC of 1970 regulates brokerage firms.

22. C

The Investment Company Act of 1940 regulates mutual funds.

23. B

The Securities Act of 1934 regulates existing securities.

24. A

The Securities Act of 1933 regulates new securities.

25. D

PV = -$4,000
FV = $7,000
i = 7
PMT = 0
n = ? = 9

26. D

The primary issuers of individual bonds are local government, state government, US government, an agency of the US government, and corporations.

27. C

Group disability benefits, monthly parking allowance, and occasional theatre tickets are tax-free fringe benefits. The allowable discount for employer-provided services is limited to 20% of the price at which the employer offers the same services to non-employees.

28. D

A plan is considered to be informally funded if the employee has no rights or secured interest in the benefit; the benefit is always subject to the claims of the company's creditors; the benefit consists of life insurance, mutual funds, or other securities; and a promise to pay is the employee's only security of future benefits.

29. B
Selling a naked call will expose an investor to the greatest amount of risk.

30. D
Ademption is the failure of a gift of property to be distributed according to the provisions of a will because the property no longer belongs to the testator at the time of death.

31. B
For EE Bond interest to be excluded from gross income, the bond must have been issued after December 31, 1989 to an individual who was at least 24 years old. The exclusion is phased out for higher income taxpayers and is not available for married taxpayers filing separately.

32. C
Begin Mode
PMT = $60,000
n = 25
i = [(1.06 / 1.08) −1] × 100 = -1.8519
FV = 0
PV = ? = $1,894,279.39

33. B
Closed-end mutual funds may sell at a premium or discount to their net asset value. Only open-end mutual funds may issue new shares when an individual buys existing shares.

34. B
Michelle has given her nephew a remainder interest in the house.

35. D
Liquidity is the ability to sell or redeem an investment quickly and at a known price without incurring a significant loss of principal. Marketability is the speed and ease with which a security may be bought or sold.

36. A
According to Principle of Professionalism, a CFP® Board designee shall return a client's original records in a timely manner after their return has been requested by the client.

37. A
Only the rental property is eligible for a like-kind exchange.

38. D
PV = -$10,500
n = 4 x 12 = 48
i = 11 / 12 = 0.9167
FV = 0
PMT = ? = $271.38

39. D
High turnover will reduce employer contributions to a defined benefit plan, especially if it leads to large forfeitures. Large forfeitures will provide more funds to pay benefits, resulting in less employer contributions.

40. D
The lifetime learning credit is available for undergraduate, graduate, and professional education expenses.

41. D
Mutual fund: Diversification smoothes price volatility, historical above-inflation return, can preserve purchasing power in a portfolio

42. A
Money market fund: Liquid, easily converted to cash, low default risk, low real return

43. B
Corporate Bond: Fixed return, may lose value if not held until maturity, fixed interest payments

44. E
Real estate: Not liquid, generally adequate inflation hedge

45. C
Common stock: Used to generate income and growth, marketable, historical above-inflation return, can preserve purchasing power in a portfolio

46. C
Chapter 7 bankruptcy involves liquidation of assets. Chapter 13 bankruptcy involves reorganization of debt.

47. B
Permitted investments in a 403b plan include mutual funds, annuity contracts, and life insurance if it is incidental to an annuity contract.

48. A
If an insured of a life insurance policy dies during the grace period and the premium has not yet been paid, the prorated premium will be subtracted from the death benefit and the remainder will be paid to the beneficiary.

49. A
Net operating losses have a two-year carry back period and a twenty-year carry forward period.

50. D
Revenue Procedures are generally related to compliance matters such as tax tables, inflation indexed amounts, and asset class lives. They deal with the procedural rather than substantive matters of tax law.

51. A
Treasury Regulations are a direct extension of the law-making powers of Congress. Next to the Internal Revenue Code, Treasury Regulations are the highest source of authority.

52. E
A Technical Advice Memorandum is guidance provided by the Office of Chief Counsel upon the request of an IRS director in response to technical questions that develop during a proceeding.

53. B
Revenue Rulings provide interpretations of tax law and give guidance to taxpayers. They are generally binding on all taxpayers.

54. C
Private Letter Rulings are specific interpretations related to the tax consequences of a transaction at the request of a taxpayer. They are only binding on the taxpayer that requests the ruling.

55. D
Timmy's income is earned, so the kiddie tax rules do not apply. A child, under age 18, who is employed by a parent in an unincorporated business, does not have to pay social security taxes.

56. B
A benefit plan is considered to be informally funded if assets are set aside in a general reserve fund to meet the benefit obligations of the plan.

57. D
No deduction is allowed for a donor's contribution of time or services to a qualified charity.

58. C

Basic Form of covered perils: HARVEST WFL

Hail, aircraft, riot, vandalism, vehicles, volcanic eruption, explosion, smoke, theft, windstorm, fire, lightning

Broad Form of covered perils: Basic Form + FAR

Falling objects, freezing pipes, artificially generated electricity, ruptured system

59. D

The married couple's personal use of the beach house can be the longer of 14 days, or 10% of the rental period. The rental period is 150 days (5 months x 30 days), so they can personally use the beach house for 15 days.

60. A

A 401k plan is a type of profit sharing plan.

61. B

A money purchase plan is a type of pension plan.

62. A

A stock bonus plan is a type of profit sharing plan.

63. A

An ESOP is a type of profit sharing plan.

64. B

A target benefit plan is a type of pension plan.

65. A

A thrift savings plan is a type of profit sharing plan.

66. B

A cash balance plan is a type of pension plan.

67. C

A terminated employee may convert a group term life insurance policy to an individual cash value policy without evidence of insurability. The premium is based on the employee's age on the conversion date.

68. B
In order for group term life insurance to be excluded from an employee's income, the coverage must provide a general death benefit which is excludible from income. The amount of insurance provided to each employee can be computed under a formula based on age, years of service, compensation, or position.

69. D
With "Option B" universal life policies, the death benefit is equal to the face amount of the policy plus the accumulation fund. The mortality charges are based on the face amount of the policy every year.

70. C
The first required minimum distribution from a traditional IRA must be taken by April 1 of the year following the calendar year in which the participant turns age 70 ½.

71. C
An asset's adjusted basis is equal to its initial cost plus expenses of sale less depreciation and amortization.

72. B
Government employers, church employers, and employers with less than 20 employees are exempt from COBRA continuation coverage.

73. C
Residential rental property has a useful life of 27.5 years.

74. B
Office equipment, except computers, has a useful life of 7 years.

75. A
Autos, light-duty trucks, and computers have a useful life of 5 years.

76. D
Commercial rental property has a useful life of 39 years.

77. C
For a qualified retirement plan to pass the percentage test, the plan must benefit at least 70% of all employees who are not highly compensated.

78. B
If a company has three owners, then six life insurance policies will be purchased if a cross-purchase agreement is used.

79. B
Employees pay a social security payroll tax of 6.2% on all wages up to the social security wage base. An additional tax of 1.45% is paid by each employee to fund Medicare, for a combined payroll tax of 7.65% for each employee.

80. D
The collateral assignment method is a type of split-dollar life insurance coverage in which the insured pays the portion of the premium that supports the death benefit, and when the insured dies the other party recovers its investment and the beneficiary receives the death benefit, less any amount owed to the other party, tax free.

81. C
An individual who gifts his or her assets to another person or entity within 5 years of applying for Medicaid will be subject to an enrollment penalty.

82. A
A life insurance policy exchanged for a life insurance policy is a permitted 1035 exchange.

83. A
An annuity exchanged for an annuity is a permitted 1035 exchange.

84. B
An annuity exchanged for a life insurance policy is <u>not</u> a permitted 1035 exchange.

85. A
A life insurance policy exchanged for an annuity is a permitted 1035 exchange.

86. D
HO-4 is a renter's policy that provides no coverage on the dwelling. It provides liability coverage and broad form coverage on personal property only.

87. C
To qualify for the Section 2032A "special use valuation", qualifying real property must have been owned by the decedent or a member of his or her family for a period of at least 5 years out of the prior 8 years ending on the date of the decedent's death.

88. A
Variable life insurance policies have fixed premiums and provide a guaranteed minimum death benefit. The cash value is linked to the performance of underlying investments, which may include the Dow Jones stock average.

89. C
A personal service corporation (PSC) cannot pass earnings or losses through to its shareholders. Any income retained by a PSC is taxed at a flat 35% rate, instead of the graduated corporate tax rates. Both S Corps and PSCs provide a step-up in basis at death, limited liability, and deductions for business expenses.

90. B
The category or risk in which loss is the only possible outcome is known as pure risk.

91. B
The trust described is a charitable remainder unitrust (CRUT) because the value of the trust is revalued annually.

92. A
The part of Medicare that pays for hospital expenses, but not physician's charges, is Medicare Part A.

93. C
Policy dividends are partly a return of a deliberate overcharge of premium by the insurer.

94. C
If property that could otherwise be valued with use of the alternate valuation date is sold prior to the six-month valuation date, the property must be valued on IRS Form 706 at its sales price.

95. C
Decreasing term life insurance is characterized by a level premium and decreasing face amount of coverage.

96. B
The annual payout rate for a CRUT must be at least 5% of the current fair market value of trust assets.

97. C
If a qualified disclaimer is made, the beneficiary that disclaims is considered to have never received the property and has not made a subsequent gift.

98. B
The three categories of hazards are moral, morale, and physical.

99. C
To be legally effective, all trusts must have a grantor, trustee, and beneficiary.

100. A
Contributions to a Roth IRA can be made at any age and are never deductible. A Roth IRA owner is not required to take a minimum distribution during his or her lifetime.

101. C
For a reverse gift, a step-up in basis is not allowed if the donee/decedent dies within 1 year of receiving a gift and then transfers the property back to the original donor.

102. C
The EAFE Index (Europe, Australia, and the Far East) is a value weighted index of the equity performance of major foreign markets.

103. B
A QDOT is not necessary if a non-citizen spouse dies first and leaves all of his or her property to a US citizen spouse.

104. C
General obligation bonds are backed by the full faith and credit of the government issuing the bonds and are repaid through taxes collected by the government body.

105. B
A QPRT is generally appropriate for vacation homes valued over $1 million. The grantor will have a taxable gift upon the creation of a QPRT.

106. D
According to the efficient market hypothesis, daily fluctuations in stock prices are a result of a random walk pattern.

107. B
Incentive stock options (ISOs) may be granted to employees only.

108. B
A living will is a legal document that allows an individual to specify wishes about medical treatment and artificial life support under specific circumstances. A living will is also known as an advance medical directive.

109. C
A profit sharing plan is a type of defined contribution plan other than a pension plan. Contributions must be substantial and recurring, but are not required annually.

110. B

Conditional receipt is evidence provided of premium payment that accompanies an application for insurance.

111. B

A first-time home purchase and qualified education expenses for a participant's child are among the exemptions from the 10% early withdrawal penalty from an IRA. Hardship withdrawals are permitted in 401k plans but not IRAs. Loans from IRAs are not allowed.

112. D

In order to make an inter-vivos gift, the donor must be legally competent; the donee must be capable of receiving and possessing the property; there must be delivery to, and acceptance by, the donee or the donee's agent; and the donor must make a "complete" gift.

113. C

In a defined contribution plan, the premiums paid for whole life insurance coverage cannot exceed 50% of the contributions made to the plan on the participant's behalf.

114. C

Unpaid interest from an annuity is considered income in respect of a decedent (IRD).

115. D

An individual is an active participant in a defined benefit plan if he or she participates or meets the eligibility requirements at any time during the plan year. Therefore, an individual is an active participant in a defined benefit plan if he or she is eligible but declines to participate.

116. C

If spouses split one gift in a calendar year, all gifts must be split. Even if no gift tax is due, a gift tax return must still be filed.

117. A

Gifts made during a donor's lifetime receive a carryover of basis, and gifts made at death receive a step-up of basis.

118. C

Modern Portfolio Theory is based on the assumption that investors are risk-averse, and for a given level of risk investors will prefer higher returns to lower returns.

119. D

Loans from a SIMPLE IRA are not permitted, but loans from a SIMPLE 401k are permitted.

120. B
Assets that transfer by contract include retirement plans and life insurance policies with beneficiary designations.

121. A
Assets that transfer by operation of law include property with survivorship rights, such as JTRWOS and tenancy by entirety.

122. A
Assets that transfer by operation of law include property with survivorship rights, such as JTRWOS and tenancy by entirety.

123. B
Assets that transfer by contract include retirement plans and life insurance policies with beneficiary designations.

124. A
Open-end mutual funds sell at their net asset value. Only closed-end mutual funds have a fixed capital structure.

125. D
The payout rate for a charitable remainder trust must be between 5% at a minimum and 50% at a maximum.

126. B
REIT shareholders are not subject to double taxation.

127. D
Defensive stocks are unaffected by general fluctuations in the economy. They include food, tobacco, and oil stocks.

128. A
The defined benefit plan, target benefit plan, and cash balance plan all favor older employees. The money purchase plan favors younger employees.

129. B
A donee's basis is increased by any gift tax paid. When a donor's basis exceeds the fair market value of the property, the donee has two bases. One basis is for subsequent gain, and the other is for subsequent loss.

130. D

The standard expiration period for a put or call option is 9 months. Long-term equity anticipation securities (LEAPS) have an expiration period longer than 1 year.

131. A

ERISA requires plan sponsors to disclose full and accurate information about qualified retirement plan activity to all participants.

132. D

Crummey powers provide a beneficiary with a right of withdrawal equal to the lesser of the amount of the gift tax annual exclusion or the value of the gift transferred.

133. D

Risk is eliminated when the correlation coefficient between two securities is -1.

134. A

For incentive stock options (ISOs), an employee must be employed by the same company without interruption from the time the option is granted until 3 months or less before the date of exercise.

135. C

If a seller dies during the installment period of an installment sale, the present value of any future payments yet to be received by the seller are included in the seller's gross estate. If the seller survives the installment period, the property sold is excluded from the seller's gross estate.

136. B

If an investment is held for more than one year, the holding period return overstates the true investment return on an annual basis. If an investment is held for less than one year, the holding period return understates the true return.

137. A

ADR dividends are declared in local currencies and paid in US dollars.

138. D

HPR = [($7,000 + $300) - $5,000] / $5,000
HPR = $2,300 / $5,000
HPR = 46%

139. B

For incentive stock options (ISOs), if the fair market value of the stock exceeds $100,000 at the time of grant, the amount in excess of $100,000 is treated as an NQSO with different tax treatment.

140. D
A standard power of attorney lapses when the principal or agent dies, or when the principal becomes mentally incapacitated.

141. A
Because they are growing and expanding, growth stocks typically do not pay large dividends. Most of the earnings generated from growth stocks are reinvested back into the company.

142. D
IRAs may invest in all four types of investments, including real estate (REITs).

143. C
A CRAT can pay Tyler a fixed percentage of the initial fair market value of the trust. With a CRUT, the annual payout would be based on the fair market value of the trust revalued annually.

144. A
Book value = total assets − (intangible assets + liabilities)

145. B
A death benefit only (DBO) plan is a type of deferred compensation plan under which all benefits are payable upon death to the beneficiaries designated by the employee. It can be funded through life insurance or it can represent accumulated deferred compensation of an employee over plan years on an unfunded basis.

146. B
According to the anomaly known as the P/E effect, low P/E stocks appear to outperform high P/E stocks over annual periods after being adjusted for risk and size.

147. B
In order to qualify for social security disability benefits, a worker must be unable to perform any substantial gainful activity.

148. D
If a wash sale occurs, no loss deduction is allowed, and the amount of the disallowed loss is added to the cost basis of the newly acquired shares.

149. D
Under the social security system, a fully insured worker is one that has paid into the system for at least 40 quarters during his or her employment career.

150. B
Sharpe ratio = (0.15 - 0.04) / 0.07
Sharpe ratio = 1.57

151. B
A group term life insurance policy can be converted to an individual life policy within 31 days of an employee terminating employment.

152. A
According to the Arbitrage Pricing Theory, security prices in different markets will not differ for any significant period of time.

153. B
The employee can retire at age 63 ½ and receive COBRA continuation coverage for 18 months. The question states the employee works for a large company, so it can reasonably be assumed the company has twenty or more employees. At age 65, the individual will be eligible for Medicare.

154. C
The S&P index has non-diversifiable risk. Non-diversifiable risk is also referred to as systematic risk.

155. A
In order to use the marital deduction, there may be a requirement that the surviving spouse survive the decedent for a period not to exceed six months.

156. A
The coefficient of variation for Security A is 1.11 (0.10 / 0.09 = 1.11). The coefficient of variation for Security B is 1.60 (0.08 / 0.05 = 1.60). A risk-averse investor would select Security A because it has a lower coefficient of variation.

157. C
In order for a spouse to waive her right to a pre-retirement survivor annuity and a joint and survivor annuity, a written waiver must be signed and witnessed by a notary or by an official of the plan. Once the waiver is signed, it is irrevocable.

158. C
Covariance = 0.30 x 6.5 x 12.4
Covariance = 24.18

159. D
All of the individuals listed are eligible for health coverage without the cost of the premium being included in the employee's income.

160. B

The lower a bond's interest rate, the greater its relative price fluctuation. The longer a bond's term to maturity, the greater its relative price fluctuation.

161. A

A 401k plan is a qualified plan, but a 403b plan is not a qualified plan.

162. B

Mortgage REITs invest in loans secured by real estate.

163. C

A REMIC is a self-liquidating, flow-through entity that invests in real estate mortgages or mortgage-backed securities.

164. A

Equity REITs acquire ownership interests in commercial, industrial, and residential properties. Income is received from the rental of these properties.

165. B

A defined benefit plan favors older owner/employees and would provide the greatest retirement benefit to Mark.

166. D

The basic types of coverage provided by long-term care policies are skilled nursing care, intermediate nursing care, home health care, custodial care, assisted living, adult day care, and hospice care.

167. C

A SEP and SARSEP require immediate vesting. A money purchase plan and 403b plan may select alternate vesting schedules.

168. A

Buying a call and selling a put are bullish strategies. Investors choose these options when they expect the stock market to rise.

169. C

A special catch up provision is permitted in 403b plans for employees with at least 15 years of service who have not made contributions and are employed by universities.

170. C

A QTIP trust provides the decedent/grantor's estate with the unlimited marital deduction while, at the same time, ensuring the decedent retains control over the ultimate disposition of his or her property.

171. C

A loss on the sale of securities is not deductible if a taxpayer purchases identical securities within 30 days prior to or after the date of sale. This is referred to as the wash sale rule.

172. B

Money purchase plan: A plan that requires a fixed percentage of compensation to be contributed for each eligible employee.

173. D

Target benefit plan: A plan similar to a defined benefit plan because contributions are based on projected retirement benefits.

174. A

Profit sharing plan: A type of defined contribution plan that is not a pension plan.

175. C

Cash balance plan: A defined benefit plan that defines an employee's benefit in terms that are more characteristic with a defined contribution plan.

176. C

According to the Principle of Objectivity, a CFP® Board designee shall exercise reasonable and prudent professional judgment in providing professional services to clients.

177. B

In a defined benefit plan, the employer assumes the investment risk.

178. D

By adding a sprinkling provision to a trust, a grantor is allowing for certain future financial circumstances among beneficiaries that he or she cannot foresee at the present time.

179. D

Legal expenses incurred by a taxpayer in connection with being represented in a tax audit are deductible. Legal expenses incurred by a taxpayer in connection with defending title to a property are non-deductible.

180. B

In a QDOT, the non-citizen surviving spouse must receive all of the income from the trust.

181. B

COBRA continuation coverage is provided to employees who are voluntarily or involuntarily terminated for reasons except gross misconduct.

182. D
Interest earned on private activity bonds is a tax preference item for AMT.

183. B
In order to use the Section 121 exclusion, a taxpayer must satisfy the ownership test and the use test.

184. D
Meals are excluded from an employee's gross income if they are provided by the employer, on the employer's premises, and for the convenience of the employer.

185. C
Treasury bills have maturities of 1 year or less.
Treasury notes have maturities of 10 years or less.
Treasury bonds have maturities greater than 10 years.

186. A
The gift tax annual exclusion is permitted for present interest gifts only.

187. B
Viatical payments to a terminally ill insured are non-taxable if he or she has a life expectancy of two years or less.

188. A
A secular trust is an irrevocable trust set up by an employer to provide nonqualified benefits to an employee. Employer contributions to a secular trust are not subject to the claims of the company's creditors.

189. D
403b plan participants may include public school employees, not-for-profit hospital employees, and church employees.

190. A
In a long call, the maximum gain is unlimited and the maximum loss is the premium.

191. A
An individual can avoid paying the excise tax for over contributing to an IRA if he or she withdrawals the excess contribution and earnings before the due date of the federal income tax return.

192. A
A trustee is the legal owner of trust property. A trustee must act at all times for the exclusive benefit of the beneficiaries or he or she may incur a legal liability. A trustee has a fiduciary duty to all trust beneficiaries regardless of whether they are income or remainder beneficiaries.

193. B

A bond's coupon rate is the stated annual interest rate that will be paid each period for the term of a bond. It is stated as a percentage of the face value of the bond.

194. B

An IRA must be created and funded by April 15 of the calendar year following the year in which the contribution applies.

195. D

Tenancy by entirety is a form of joint tenancy allowed only for married couples.

196. B

Basic Form of covered perils: HARVEST WFL

Hail, aircraft, riot, vandalism, vehicles, volcanic eruption, explosion, smoke, theft, windstorm, fire, lightning

Broad Form of covered perils: Basic Form + FAR

Falling objects, freezing pipes, artificially generated electricity, ruptured system

197. D

A 3-for-1 stock split will decrease a stock's market price per share. A reverse stock split will increase a stock's market price per share.

198. C

For ADRs, banks collect money in their local currency and then convert to US dollars.

199. D

A rabbi trust may become irrevocable if there is a change in corporate control. The trust creates security for employees because the assets in the trust are outside the employer's control.

200. A

A family limited partnership can be used to reduce an individual's gross estate, and therefore, reduce estate taxes.

ABOUT THE AUTHOR

Matthew Brandeburg is a certified financial planner and President of Bridgeway Financial Group, LLC in Columbus, Ohio. Along with advising families and small businesses across the country, Matthew is the author of the books "Financial Planning For Your First Job", "Your Guide to the CFP® Certification Exam", and "CFP® Certification Exam Practice Question Workbook". In addition, Matthew teaches the course "Financial Planning in your 20s and 30s" at Ohio State University.

INDEX

Made in the USA
Charleston, SC
05 January 2012